T0367946

FOCUStrategy

Also by John Canavan

www.focustrategy.com

Navigating Your Professional Growth

John Canavan

ISBN: 978-1-4525-5449-5 (sc)
ISBN: 978-1-4525-5479-2 (e)
ISBN: 978-1-4525-5450-1 (hc)

Library of Congress Control Number: 2012911431

Balboa Press books may be ordered through booksellers or by contacting:

Balboa Press
A Division of Hay House
1663 Liberty Drive
Bloomington, IN 47403
www.balboapress.com
1-(877) 407-4847

Printed in the United States of America

Balboa Press rev. date: 06/27/2012

To my father, Michael Canavan,
who continues to guide me.

To my mother, Lucy Canavan,
who inspires me.

To my friend Max Falk,
who continues to mentor me.

Contents

Introduction

The office has a social fluency that demands your constant awareness. If you are looking to grow professionally, your smarts just are not enough. You need to be able to navigate the interoffice and business environment. There are competing interests, ideas, politics, and motives. Miscalculating will set you back.

FocuStrategy is not designed to teach you or bombard you with details. It's designed to make you think, to provoke your ideas, and to keep you moving forward. Only you know the variables and intricacies—based on your own perspective—of the business or position you are in. What works for one does not always work for another. Personalities vary to such a degree that your perspective and strategy will differ from that of anyone else. Why would you use someone else's formula, just to have it backfire? You're smarter than that, and there are way too many variables and possibilities for you to allow yourself to be led.

Once you cease to understand and compete, you jeopardize your momentum and risk falling behind. Attempting to catch up at that point is exhausting. (Think of NASCAR—if you pit for a blowout, good luck making it back to your spot.) This is true both as an overall business strategy and on an interoffice level. Turnarounds are tough and take a long time.

They involve capital—both monetary and human—and they involve in-depth strategic planning, creativity, innovation, evaluations, and much more. If we're talking about you as an individual, much of the same applies. You've fallen behind, made mistakes—you need a self-turnaround.

Look, we are all just trying to make it through. Dealing with subordinates, colleagues, and bosses requires a strategy. Whatever is happening out there is not the other person's fault—it's up to you to be focused, to be nimble, to be creative, to be prepared, and to have a strategy to take you from here to there through all the challenges in between.

If I had to write a phrase to describe every heading in this book, it would be, "*Do not stay still.*"

1

Manage Your Time

Time management is something that's easier described than done. How many times have you attempted to budget your time and failed? It takes a lot of focus to keep from going over or under—and either way, you do not achieve what you want. Time management is essential to your ability to progress in a deliberate and organized manner.

If, for example, you're working on a project and do not have a grasp of how to budget your time, you'll find yourself actually wasting it. Time is a perishable commodity—you will never get it back. Not only will that particular project be slowed, but so will your overall progress.

This is not to say that some things don't take time to work on or complete. But having a strategy and focusing on time will make a difference. Think of some of the people you work with who you must constantly revisit or contact for additional information or other things. They are wasting your time because they are not managing theirs.

2

Be Decisive

Making decisions sounds easy enough, but it's not always. A situation often comes up in which you're either afraid to make a decision or you think you need to check with your supervisor, directors, board members, and so on—when, in reality, others want *you* to make the decision. Why? Because it saves them from having to make it and allows them to focus on more pressing issues. Of course, there are matters that require some deliberation. Your judgment is important here. Ultimately, though, there's nothing more impressive than someone taking the initiative to make a decision.

3

Run Meetings Efficiently

Keep meetings to the point and get them over with quickly because no one likes them. Preparation is one of the keys to running meetings. An agenda can help you stay on track, but because variables always present themselves, it's difficult to hold a meeting within a concise timeframe. This shouldn't stop you from trying.

Understanding what you are trying to get out of a meeting and what points you are attempting to make allows you to set the pace. Everyone has his or her own style and management techniques, so creating a consistent and predictable format allows others to be more prepared.

One thing you don't want to do in meetings—especially with six or more attendees—is get bogged down in discussions that pertain to only a few. Discussions headed in that direction should be cut off, and a separate, more focused meeting on that topic should be scheduled.

4

Get to Know Potential Employees

Hiring is a trip into the great unknown, no matter how much research and background-checking you do. If the potential employee is going to work directly for you, the best thing you can do is converse with the individual. His or her mannerisms will give you the core information you need to make an assessment on a personal level. This doesn't mean you're going to go out clubbing with this person, but you want him or her to have your interests in mind. We are not cyborgs; we are social by nature, and we need to feel comfortable enough to manage, delegate, and work through issues without personality conflicts.

Testing for specific answers within a hiring matrix is good, but it shouldn't be the complete basis for hiring. Some people know how to work the answers, and those are the kind of unnatural and deceptive individuals you really want to stay away from. They may become derailers or outright troublemakers who will lower morale and stifle creativity. The saying "One bad apple spoils the bunch" didn't come out of nowhere. There's a reason for it.

Now, how do you go through the process of hiring? Yes, have your hiring matrix prepared and complete the scoring in the traditional manner. Once you've completed that, though, lighten up the interview. Some people are very nervous in interviews and actually perform much better in a less formal environment. There's nothing wrong with that. Other people perform well under pressure. Either way, it's good to have both tracks available to assess the candidate and bring in the right person.

Initiate a more personal conversation within the context of the business, something to the effect of what the candidate is proud of, what his or her references and people close to him or her would say, and what kind of passion the person has for business or the position. What kind of details are involved in what the candidate is describing? Having the potential employee elaborate will give you insight into how he or she sees things, and hence how that person may perform on the job.

5

Encourage Innovation

If you're not innovating, you are falling behind. There's much to say about this topic, but the bottom line is that the ideas must keep flowing, and whether you implement many or few, you must at least be discussing potential innovations. Many companies will simply copy another's innovation. Honestly, there's nothing wrong with that; they save a lot of capital. And that in itself can be a form of innovation—perhaps to enhance the product or service.

In any event, if you don't have the imagination or creativity yourself, find those who do and discuss ideas with them. Imagination, creativity, innovation—these are what keep things moving.

Create a culture of innovation within your company. It's one of the first principles of having a successful business. The leaders of a company, department, project, and so on need to foster a creative environment. Without it, you have the normal, mundane, day-to-day, business-as-usual mentality that simply oppresses and suppresses any kind of motivation to generate ideas and innovate. It's deliberate persistence. It's the difference between Apple and everyone else.

6

Avoid Micromanagement

One of the worst things you can do is micromanage. It's an ego-driven process and a setup for failure. Type A personalities are good, but they are the best candidates for making this mistake. Okay, you know everything, but you don't know *everything*. Bring the details to the surface, but don't overanalyze to the point where the bigger picture becomes obscured because you're obsessing over something that someone else should be handling. Micromanaging is an annoyance to others and actually stifles growth by minimizing contrary ideas, which is never a good thing.

7

Look Out for Leaders

There's a saying that being critical of a situation is a sign of intelligence. My guess is that this comes from the difference between a leader—someone who thinks—and the led—a sheep, basically, accepting and moving through situations without much thought.

I'm not saying this is true in every case, but if there's an employee showing some unhappiness with the status quo, chances are that employee is smart and ambitious. This is the type of person you want pushing things through. Sometimes these people need training and refinement, but the cost is worth it. Would you rather settle for sheep who are more interested in maintaining than producing?

8

Understand the Particulars

When meeting with subordinates, it is important that your executive committee and managers—whether in private meetings, group meetings, board meetings, or executive-committee meetings—listen to and understand the particulars of what is said and asked. It must be communicated that if these leaders are unsure of what is being said or required, they must feel comfortable and confident enough to ask. Policies and procedures are considered and made based on many variables that impact clients, employees, and operations. No department is isolated, segregated, or autonomous.

The particulars of what is said are important. Distinguishing between what is being communicated and the ideas behind that communication is critical. Is it a directive, suggestion, or recommendation? Again, the listener must be sure, as that is the only way the policy or procedure will be implemented properly.

What happens when people make assumptions? The action or remedy that is assumed results in other actions based only on an assumption; hence, other actions and presumed remedies are carried out under a false belief. Time is wasted, additional meetings are necessary, and productivity, policies, procedures are inefficient or delayed.

A deliberate momentum must be the norm. Otherwise, we are simply maintainers and not managers. Listen to the particulars of what is said.

9

Empower Your Employees

Most people—though not all—like to be challenged. It's nice to come home from work or play and have a story to tell about something you've accomplished. One of the most important things to keep in mind when managing is that you do not have a monopoly on ideas. Acting as if you do is arrogant and, at a minimum, will suppress creativity and competitiveness. When you empower employees to make suggestions, it gives them an opportunity to be a part of the organization, encourages quick and strategic thinking, and allows you to set and meet priorities. Give them the reasons, and allow them to create the agenda to get there.

10

Devise a Turnaround Strategy

Turning around an organization that is in deep trouble is probably one of the toughest things to accomplish. It can be done, but you must stay focused on a strategy. The key points are austerity; cost containment; crisis challenge; transformation and opportunity; proper staff; and radical changes. Let's take them one by one.

Austerity

What does this mean? Stop spending! When you know how to do something a certain way—when it's fixed in your brain—one of the hardest things to do is to change that process. For example, once you've traveled first class on a plane, it's difficult to go back to coach. Once you've driven a foreign luxury car or sports car, it's very difficult to make the switch to a lesser vehicle. But austerity means to stop spending on the things you can stop spending on, and seek alternatives or eliminate them. It's not easy, but you must do it.

Cost Containment

This is different from austerity. Cost containment refers to everything from labor and related costs to just-in-time purchasing to stretching dollars through smart managing of all costs. The trick here is to not sacrifice quality. Your clients will be able to tell in a moment, and you will then lose the most critical element to your survival.

Crisis Challenge

Yes, it's a crisis, and you are being challenged. While you're in a turnaround mode, all aspects of the business must be scrutinized and assessed (not overanalyzed). The word *crisis* demands that your attention be focused. The word *challenge* demands that you confront with honesty the predicament you are in—and believe me, if you are involved in a turnaround, you are in a predicament. A key way out is to take on the challenge in crisis mode, which allows you to create ways of strategizing your business to profitability.

Transformation and Opportunity

How are you transforming? Out of what you were and what got you here in the first place. What's the opportunity? A new way to conduct your business with a creative, innovative and focused strategy. Again, if you're in a position that you're even considering turnaround, the business needs to be transformed, and this very initiative creates opportunity. Opportunity opens all kinds of doors, and when looked at with flexibility in thought and change in mind, a bologna sandwich can actually be changed. Just think through it.

Proper Staff

Whether you have employees or you alone are the staff, either way, it has to be *proper.* What does this mean? Everyone must be in the same frame of mind, or a turnaround just won't happen. You can't have someone working against you, and you can't work against yourself. This is not to suggest that you have a derailer on staff, but it may suggest that the staff is not grasping the crisis or even the term *turnaround.* Everyone must feel empowered to share in the ideas, creativity, passion, innovation, and sacrifice. Your staff, including yourself, will make or break you in this situation. Get rid of people who will not help you through, as it makes no sense to keep them on.

Radical Changes

A radical shake-up is called for, from your marketing to your service or product to the culture of your business. Making a radical change doesn't mean doing a 360 wrapped differently; it means doing a 180 in a better wrapping. You need to figure it out. Think!

If you're in a turnaround, you've lost your way. You can find your way back by thinking and working through the steps above. They don't give you the complete answers or the Holy Grail, but they are an important part of a focused strategy. None of what you do will show results immediately. It's a slow, grueling process, with setbacks, insecurities, and self-pity. But slow and steady wins the race.

11

Be Innovative

To be innovative, you must anticipate what customers want and what kind of values apply—and then have the flexibility to make the slightest changes when that want and value point need refining. When innovation is taken seriously, it creates a momentum of its own. One idea feeds off another idea, leading to more questions and then answers. The momentum is undeniable. You're constantly moving forward in some way. What's the one constant in the world? Change. Innovation is change. It's important to your business because it shows clients and customers that management is thinking and acting with care.

12

Set the Tone

When dealing with staff, how do you make your approach? It's a very important matter, because you will set the tone for future interactions and directives. Have you ever heard it said that we all act in accordance with our surroundings? What this means is that people act differently depending on who they are interacting with. Sometimes it's subtle and hard to detect, but other times it's not so subtle. The point is that if you set a "Mr. Softy" tone right from the beginning, it will be difficult to get control afterward; once your staff has started to take advantage, it's almost impossible to reverse the process, and unfair to the employee who you allowed to get the upper hand in the first place.

Of course, you also don't want to go in like it's Gestapo headquarters. That would destroy morale and suppress any creative thinking before you can even say the word *tone*.

So what's the right approach? Understand your staff members and their talents and weaknesses. What you're trying to do is find a fit, and adjust your approach to that fit within your organization or department. Your tone in dealing with these talents will create a culture that allows you to manage effectively. You need to go in tough and somewhat aloof, but not to the point at which they feel uncomfortable and unsure. There should be consistency, predictability, and firmness. That's the tone.

Intelligent people know when you're not sincere and lack leadership skills. Intelligent people do not like to be spoken to in a condescending manner, like "Great job!" Praise is good, but not in that fashion. What they want, like, and need is a leader who sets a tone of respect and high expectations.

One last thing about tone is to be careful of the more progressive approaches that some business schools are pushing. Command and control are definitely out—that's a good thing for all sorts of reasons. But the "we are the world and like to be pampered and coddled, so don't correct me harshly" approach is not correct either.

13

Prepare for Change

Change needs a strategy. Change is a talent, an art. How do you do this? How do you know when change is necessary? Knowing is instinctive. There are so many variables that can or cannot describe when change is required that it would be unfair and disingenuous to give examples in that sort of detail. Whatever the signals or thought going into it, doing it involves a plan. You need to know the basis or reason for the change and the likely outcomes once the change is made. It's like a balloon: squeeze one end, and it fills the other end. The other term for that is *cause and effect.* When making changes, some are small and in no need of a committee meeting, like changing the toilet-paper brand. You need to use you judgment.

14

Resist Complacency

Complacency is your enemy. It suggests a standstill, being stuck in neutral. You can use whatever term you want for it, but the bottom line is that if you're complacent you will fall behind, and your position—whether as a business owner, manager, or CEO—will be called into question or worse. You always have to know what you're thinking; you always have to be asking questions. Human beings are lazy by nature, so it takes a strong will and mind to break or stay away from complacency. Looking for things to improve your department, division, company, product, or service is a necessary constant. If you become complacent in your efforts, I promise your subordinates will as well. Remember, if you're not growing, you're dying.

15

Learn How to Delegate

Do you delegate, or do you hoard work because you believe you are the smartest person in the room and no one can do it as efficiently as you? Or maybe you're just trying to hold on to your importance. Have you ever heard the expression, "The cemetery is filled with indispensable people"? Believe me, the sun will rise tomorrow without you. My point is to delegate as much as you can for a great number of reasons—the biggest one being, if you are that smart, you should be working on developing ideas to improve things. By delegating, you allow many projects to take place at the same time, which you control on a more umbrella-type level.

16

Channel Passion Properly

Passion can work two ways. It can be a negative if you are blinded by it. I know, there's an expression about that, and there's a reason for it. When you're starting a business or project, you need to pull your emotions out of it. Blind passion will propel you forward into a brick wall. On the other hand, if you're passionate about something and channel it properly—leaving excitement and depression out of it—you have a much better chance of success. Move forward with a deliberate momentum, but control any emotions that involve euphoria or doubt; allow your mind to exploit the positive or the negative for purposes of adjustment.

17

Contemplate All Outcomes

An underrated strength of human beings, contemplation is different from just thinking about a situation with the usual question, "What can I do?" Contemplation means thinking through an issue from start to finish, running it through your head with all the effects and variables. It's focusing on a strategy to influence an outcome. By contemplating, you effectively prepare yourself for all outcomes, positive and negative, allowing an action to follow—one of your choosing, under your control.

I'm not suggesting that everything *must* contemplated. It takes an intelligent and experienced mind to make the quick and accurate decisions that are required in business. What I am suggesting is that the more strategy-based decisions—such as marketing initiatives, operational changes, and product or service enhancements or adjustments—require a more contemplative approach.

18

Cut Your Losses

You've often heard the expression *cut your losses*, but it's not so easy for people to do. Your stock is down, and you just won't cut your losses and accept the inevitable. It's the same with starting a business, starting a project, initiating a turnaround, creating a new product or service ... you have to know when to cut your losses. How do you do this? Well, the first way is to cut your emotions. Your emotions are unpredictable and careless. Once that's done, listen to your logic and instincts. You know when it's time to cut your losses, but you may be too arrogant, selfish, embarrassed, or angry to do so. These are all emotions, by the way.

The problem with not accepting that you have to break away is that the longer you hold on, resisting the inevitable, the more money and resources in time and labor you waste. It's bad enough if you're doing it to yourself; it's worse if someone else's time and money is involved. Try defending your position in front of your board, investors, division head—or worse, your spouse.

So, let's ask the question again: "How do you know when to cut your losses?" Mounting monetary losses is one way, but a sure sign is the feeling of struggling. If the momentum is just not there, or every decision seems to be a problem or a disconnect, you have to know the difference between a logical setback and a bad idea. It's that simple.

Now the truth is that it may just be a good idea gone bad. There are many who will argue this point and recommend "don't give up" as the answer. Really? Well, when it's not their money or time, it's easy to talk. Maybe the idea or purchase or whatever is good; let's say that's the case for argument's sake. Then perhaps it's the staff, the consumer, or the product or service that's missing one small element—it does not matter. If the numbers are not there, it's failing, and you must cut your losses and try again later. That's the beauty of numbers: they are very specific and compound up or down quickly. You either have cash flow and profitability, or you don't.

What I don't want to do is give the impression that at the first sign of struggle or red on your P&L, it's time to get out. You need a strategy and focus to make things right, but after enough time has gone by (and you'll know when that is), the tough decision must be made for everyone's sake.

19

Share Control

Control is important, but it's also important to release it when necessary. When would that be? Once you've delegated the project or task. If you're going to breathe down a subordinate's neck, you might as well do the job yourself … and then why would you need that person in the first place? (This goes to hiring and the talent pool, but that's another topic.)

Allow the talents of others to shine so that you can move on. Too much control is bad for morale and stifles growth. Your employees, staff, or team should be accountable, so benchmarks should be set, and you should be able to monitor them from a distance. Meetings are boring but necessary. Make them micro-meetings.

20

Cancel Compounding

Once a project, task, or company is set in a bad direction, losses begin to compound. *Compound*: hold that word. Another term, *turnaround manager/expert*, comes from someplace, and it's when things have compounded so badly in the wrong direction that it's necessary to attempt to save a company from the inevitable. It's very hard to do, and you do not want to be in that position. The whole basis of the title of this book is *not* to get into this position. Focus on a strategy from the beginning, and adjust it when required. Know your stuff; know your numbers; know your people's talents.

21

Engage in Self-Analysis

Take a look at yourself and the position or job you're doing, whether it's owning a business or managing a team or department. Is this what you really want to do? Do you have the equilibrium for it, or did you just fall into it? Do you just flow with the everyday responsibilities and basically maintain the status quo? There's a point to these questions: if you are not reading to educate yourself, or keeping up on your industry's movements and future, you are not doing anyone any good—including yourself—by continuing to do what you do. Get out, move over, and let someone who cares do what needs to be done. It sounds harsh and easy, but imagine for a moment that you are doing something you really want to do. Instead of giving it 50 percent or 80 percent, you would give 100 percent with little effort.

(Now, you may be doing what you like and want to do, but have a poor manager or owner who's the complete opposite of what this book is about. That's another topic.)

Self-analysis is critical for many reasons, but the main reason is to realize your need to read and educate yourself constantly for the good of the businesses you are in and for yourself. On this topic, I'll leave you with this: I was speaking to a young woman of twenty-nine years old who said to me that she felt she was falling behind on technology. You don't want to fall behind on anything just because you have a comfortable feeling things are okay at the moment. What's the expression? If you're not moving forward, you're dying?

22

Keep Having Ideas

Ideas are pulled from many different sources. The key is to keep having them. Sure, some will be bad, some ridiculous, some odd. But some will be good, and you'll never know that unless you work through the idea.

You need a constant supply of ideas. They are signs of an active mind, they work your creative right hemisphere, and they develop the imagination Albert Einstein was so fond of.

Where do ideas come from? Everywhere. Every time you pick up a book (and read it of course), every time you discuss a topic, every time you contemplate an issue or problem, you are generating ideas. Capture them, contemplate them, and act on them. They make the difference between a doer and, well, a non-doer who's on the road to nowhere at high speed.

23

Sharpen Your Strategies

Strategic sharpening is a way of putting attention toward your plan or strategy, but focusing, fine-tuning, and adjusting to keep it sharpened with less of a chance for errors or unintended consequences. *Sharpening* suggests that something has gone dull, and this is what happens with strategies and business plans, or any plan for that matter. However, it's not as simple as just adjusting or sharpening. You're not going to sharpen what does not need sharpening. The information you receive from your executive committee, directors, board, and line staff is critical. Although I've mentioned the importance of delegating, it's important to receive information and feedback pertaining to your strategy. This way, you're involved at some level and can sharpen where and when necessary.

24

Create a Functional Corporate Culture

Sometimes corporate cultures are good, and they work. Take a look at IBM—it's a textbook example. But many times, culture is a company's own worst enemy. It's like a dysfunctional family; you've identified the problems, but good luck trying to change or purge behavior.

Problems with culture can come in many forms, but for our purposes the question is, how do you work with and within a dysfunctional culture? You come into a company or a department and right away you notice inefficiencies (that will reflect on you, by the way, if you don't fix them), a less-than-cooperative staff, and the pretense of wanting to change but an underlying attitude of "Why should we?"

This is something that must be balanced very carefully and with an understanding that it will take time—and more time, depending on the size of the company or department. Many times it's not just a matter of changing policies and procedures. There are other resisting factors that need consideration, such as clients and satellite offices.

How do you effect changes? The answer is leadership and tough-ability. Work within the culture itself to change the direction. Find out the individual strengths of your team members and build on them. A redistribution of responsibilities can work like magic when each individual gains a purpose, understands a direction, and likes what he or she is doing. On the other hand, you need a strong and tough character to pull this off. If your employees see you as a marshmallow, you'll have trouble getting results. I'm not suggesting that you create an environment similar to Gestapo headquarters, but you certainly need strong leadership, no fear, and a clear vision of the outcome you seek. Be careful of more contemporary business ideologists that speak of cooperation, friendliness, and "can't we all just get along" models. Don't worry, Generation D, H, or Z (whatever we're in now) will conform. If they don't, allow them the opportunity to start their own business that they can run and manage however they like.

25

Retain Your Best People

Is retention always best? Not really. Your business should always have succession plans in place, or at minimum a clear strategy so that any key employees who depart either voluntarily or otherwise can be replaced, allowing the company to function with a predictable direction. You know the saying, "The cemetery is filled with indispensable people."

That said, there should also be policies in place to retain your best people. Paying attention to your people can help. Making sure they are challenged and content with what they do is important. (This goes back to knowing your employees.) Of course, there are circumstances in which you won't be able to retain them, but at least you tried. Remember, when people are happy in their position, they tend to perform better and are less apt to be job-searching. Something else to remember, though, is that most are not as qualified as they think they are.

26

Train Yourself

Are you trained for the position you currently hold or are seeking? Did you know that you are not as qualified as you think you are? Accomplishments, tasks, hypotheticals, knowledge, understanding, experience—all of these really just come down to theory. You are in a position, and you find yourself floating or maintaining, and the real understanding of the impact of your decisions or non-decisions simply dissipates in time. In other words, proper training allows engaging and self-starting. Being trained does not mean having the company train you in its procedures. It means training yourself through reading, studying, and attending a seminar here and there so that you are prepared for the position you occupy now or intend to occupy in the future.

Companies are looking for self-starters. Do you know how much it costs to train someone? This is why the interview process is becoming more focused. Training yourself gives you an advantage. It allows for the more strategic and creative approach that businesses want and need.

Now, what if you're starting your own business? You'd better be trained and a self-starter, because I promise no one will help you. A good idea is not enough. It's one of the biggest mistakes entrepreneurs make. Train yourself thoroughly, and do not rely on others to get you started.

27

Beware of Envy

There's a difference between being jealous and being envious. Jealousy sounds stronger, but ultimately it's more of an immature emotion that creates a sort of quick bad taste about someone or something. Envy is much more in-depth. When we are envious of someone or something, it may ferment and create distractions because of unfocused and unrealistic thinking. In other words, if you're envious of another's position—whether a person or a corporate entity—that envy becomes a tenacious blocker of clear thought and strategy. Your decisions are murky, impacting performance on many levels.

Is this something that can be easily dismissed? There are many whose constitution is not strong enough to remove this element, and they make manipulative decisions that create stealth problems. Beware of your own envious thoughts and the envious behavior of others.

28

Catch Up

How do you catch up when you've fallen behind? Create a strategy and focus on it like a laser. This is a distressing position to be in, whether it's you personally or your organization. Catch-up requires you to quickly learn what went wrong and investigate what your competitors (personal or corporate) have done right; create a strategy (not expecting it to work overnight); and implement all of this at an efficient speed. It's akin to the last few seconds in a football game where the losing team is hurrying down the field. Your competitors are not standing still and have the advantage, so a meticulous strategy is imperative to catching up.

29

Respond to Issues Appropriately

Not everything requires a response, and sometimes it's just as important to dismiss an "issue" and move on. This is something that should be thought out with clarity. An issue may seem important on the surface, but calculating quickly whether a particular issue is worth your time and response is critical to your next step. Think about it: issues are going to crop up constantly, and if you're wasting your time on an issue that will bear no benefit, then why are you dealing with it? Because you think it requires a response, or are you simply being mechanical?

The suggestion here is to not walk around assessing and analyzing whether this or that needs a response, but get in the habit of quick thinking on whether it's necessary.

On the other side of this is the absolute necessity of a response that will help steer the process to your position. Think of it as a plane's navigation system, constantly adjusting and compensating for variances in thinks like wind or speed.

The larger point with Issue Response is finding ways to incorporate your responses to issues in a strategic sense. An issue is an opportunity. It's actually evidence of a problem, challenge, or matter that needs attention, and it forces your thought process to overcome and problem-solve, ultimately enhancing your position.

30

Embrace Social Media

Humans are social beings. This is why when you're on a train or bus, at an airport, or wherever, your eyes are constantly moving and scanning others. It's what we are and what we do. Yes, you'll have those who will say, "I like to be alone." That may be true, but I bet they have a cell phone or a Facebook page.

The point is, your presence on social networks is growing. Information about you grows every time you hit "enter" on your keypad. Amex knows that you just shopped at Walmart, Piperlime knows what size shoe you wear, your prospective employer knows how many children you have, your mortgage company or landlord knows your income-to-debt ratio … get it? Utilizing social media to your advantage is critical. Monitor what's out there about you and manipulate or manage it, or it may have an impact on your life that you'll never understand.

Social media is growing because information is sought after and in high demand. From your business or personal Web page, Facebook page, Twitter feed, LinkedIn page, Xtranormal blog, credit-card usage, and more, your online identity will determine your future, whether you're prepared for it or not. Be prepared. Manage it.

31

Use Power Wisely

Power is a tool for cause and influence, and certainly it can be used in an abusive manner. However, if you're moral compass is set correctly, it can be used in the most effective way.

Depending on your level of power, the ability to cause disruption or a correction is determined by how much you are respected, feared, or liked by your team, colleagues, or leaders. *Cause* is more of an unintended movement of something. You've caused it to happen by saying something or acting a certain way. It's important to be aware of your power. Say something, do something, react a certain way, and watch what happens—your actions may send a project, policy, or procedure in an unintended direction.

Influence is something different. Being aware of your power and its influence can allow you to manipulate a matter in an *intended* way. Is there anything wrong with that? Absolutely not. You're in a position of power and influence—the idea is to use them in a way that drives a strategy forward based on your ideals and vision. Used effectively, they allow you to cut through the inefficiencies that take place everywhere.

Either way, your character has a lot to do with how much you can effectively use your power. For example, if you're running around screaming all the time, you won't be taken seriously. If you're a marshmallow, you won't be taken seriously either. Having a strong constitution and balance is necessary to making the most of your power. Remember, you're not in a position of power by accident. Something happened somewhere along the line to place you where you are.

Now, let's talk about how to get into a position of power. It's not an easy task, because most people in power want what? Yes, more power. And they'll do almost anything to hold on to it, which will get in your way. So the way to get into power is to cause and influence your way into it. If you are focused properly on your tasks, people will notice you. By "causing" questions and efficiencies, you will bring attention to yourself and create for yourself a situation of influence. Once that attention is on you, trust builds, additional responsibilities come your way, tasks are given, and dependence forms. What does this ultimately do? It builds your experience, knowledge, and confidence. You are on your way. No kidding.

32

Avoid the Implementation Trap

Implementation is the last step of a process that involves thought, planning, and anticipation. Where's the trap? The trap is not being prepared and implementing anyway. The moment you know what you want to create, change, or solve, you need to be thinking behind and ahead to determine whether the idea itself is worth moving on. Once that's determined or confirmed, the planning and strategizing must be well thought out. Potential issues or problems should be considered. You won't be able to think of them all—trust me, the best battle plans go astray. But planning and strategizing before implementation will allow for a much smoother transition and help you avoid the trap of being stuck with a good idea going nowhere.

33

Serve Your Customer Base

Is the customer always right? Absolutely … not! The conventional wisdom is that if your thoughts deviate from this made-up imperative, you don't understand business. To the contrary—try running your business with this type of thought process, and you will find yourself out of business in no time.

Now, what is the real wisdom about the customer? First and foremost, your product or service must have a customer base. There has to be a reason why you went into business in the first place. If your demographic, marketing, price point, product, or service is wrong, of course the customer is always going to be right. On the other hand, if you are running your business (or managing your team or department) properly, customer complaints will drop and the ones that do crop up will be more manageable. The customer is only right if you are making mistakes.

34

Measure Yourself and Your Accomplishments

No one else really cares about your accomplishments. Answering to yourself, directing yourself, focusing on yourself is the only reality there is. Yes, there are things going on around you; people are judging you, people are considering you, people are rejecting you. When you've taken measure of yourself and your accomplishments, that's when your confidence kicks in and your strategic focus carries you.

Most of us are sheep. We educate ourselves, gain experience in a trade, and then coast along. It leaves us exposed and vulnerable to others' whims. If you haven't measured yourself, no worries—someone else will, and you'll find yourself plugged into something you care little about and are mediocre at, just coasting along. Who cares? You.

35

Hire Strategically

For most companies and managers, hiring is a gamble. You do what you can to vet the candidate, but once that individual is hired, many factors will influence his or her performance, from the standard set at the top to the derailer in the middle to the office culture at the base. Your employees or subordinates can make or break you, so when looking to hire someone new, you should already have agendas and procedures in place so this new hire can navigate efficiently. If individuals are hired and see disorganization, one of three things will happen:

1. They'll resign. This is probably the least expensive for you both in time and money. The downside is that you may have lost an asset. You'll never know.

2. They'll assimilate and become part of your problem, not a solution. The whole idea behind new hiring is that it enables your company or department to grow efficiently.
3. They'll stay on, but at a cost. Smart people are not stupid and will grab an opportunity when they see it. Sometimes this isn't so bad; it may cost you, but there's an ROI if they are helping.

The point and idea here is not to go into new hiring blind, simply to place a body someplace. There must be a strategic fit. Hiring people just to have to fire or lay them off later makes zero sense.

36

Provide Succession Guidance

Key positions require succession guidance. This is different from succession preparation. You've already done the preparation work for a smooth transition into the position; therefore, the next step is guidance. It's akin to implementation and maintenance. When a policy or procedure is implemented, it just doesn't stay implemented. It requires maintenance to keep it going.

Once an individual is in his or her new position, the apparatus and support must be there simultaneously. Although this sounds simple, that's not always the case, and it can make the difference between an employee's failure and success in a key position.

37

Make a Decision and Stick to It

Some of us are decisive, and some of us aren't. Have you ever been sitting at your desk or wherever, it's 11:45 a.m., and you don't know what you want to eat for lunch? You'll figure it out ten or fifteen minutes later, and then change your mind when you see the menu. That's not decisive. Decisiveness is making a decision quickly and sticking to it.

When you're running a company, department, or project, indecisiveness—especially from the top—has the potential to drain resources of money and time, and actually creates chaos (perhaps not at the *Get Smart* level) in a way that confuses staff and clients.

Decisiveness, on the other hand, creates assurance, consistency, and confidence. Even if something goes awry, the consistency that comes with a decisive action will pull forward the collective focus of whatever is being put forth.

In simpler terms, people become accustomed to your decisive nature and are attuned to it, allowing for more accurate policies, procedures, and implementation without guesswork or a confusing approach.

38

Mature Yourself to the Position

Look, I'm not your mother advising you how to carry yourself in public. But I will say that in whatever leadership position you are in, you must bear your position's title in a respectful way if you hope to be able to lead others.

To "mature yourself," you have to understand where you stand in your organization and be able to perform and delegate for optimal results. Not being aware of how you are perceived by your subordinates, peers, and bosses will slow your growth and your ability to move things forward. Regardless of management tools and technology, we are still social beings. We judge, we are envious, jealous, political, hierarchal …

If you do not take the time to mature yourself and understand this concept, it's akin to making it into a floatation device at sea (one you were smart enough to get into) but then floating aimlessly with the current.

39

Keep Your Thoughts Connected to Reality

A disconnect in thought can cause problems in a number of ways. You can have such a misunderstanding of the integral parts of a project, goal, or policy that you go off in your own direction without realizing it—going against the flow in such a way that the divergence from the original strategy or plan complicates everyone's efforts, never mind the lost time and revenue. This is why a strategy is necessary for everything. You need to look forward. Not everything will work the way you expect, and you'll need to constantly adjust. If your thoughts are disconnected from what the strategy is, you're lost.

Another disconnect in thought comes from simple disinterest. Two answers on this one: get interested, or change the dynamic of your effort so the project *does* interest you. In other words, get involved and come up with ideas that make whatever you are working on more interesting.

The overall point here is to stay focused on the strategy, or you may find yourself in a position later wondering how and why you got there.

40

Capitalize on Emotional Intelligence

Emotional intelligence is about picking up on circumstances or situations, assessing them, and processing them in a way that can bring out a less-than-confrontational stance. For example, you may be in a board meeting, budget meeting, or policy meeting, and there's a jam or disagreement impacting the progress. An attendee with more emotional intelligence may be able to pick up on something to move the process forward, such as insecurity or an interaction that provides a missing element.

This does not mean that people with emotional intelligence have some kind of superpower that allows them to call up this ability and make everything right. We all have some kind of emotion, albeit different levels of it. It just means that some are able to pick up on things in a different way—sometimes even unbeknownst to them.

How do you capitalize on something like this? You need to know your staff and yourself, trust your instincts, and look to identify the attributes and qualities of those who work for and with you. Being able to capitalize on this can give you an advantage in negotiation, delegation, and other tasks.

41

Be Deliberate in Your Leadership

People around you notice efficiency and deliberate motion. There are all kinds of obstacles when you're trying to make things happen, and your deliberate focus—whether you see the progress or not—is what counts. Managing, being creative, looking at the effects, meeting and reaching your intention all give you experience.

Dedicating your focus and strategizing the use of the tools you have—including people—will prepare and ensure your next step. Knowing who you are managing, their skills, strengths, and weaknesses, will allow you to have them focus efficiently on your objective. If someone on your team is a weak link, you are obligated to find that individual's strength and position him or her accordingly. The possibility is great that this person's particular area of responsibility is not where his or her ability is, creating a weak link.

In any event, the point is to be deliberate in your focus, deliberate in your strategy, deliberate in your understanding of your people and your tools. You're leading to an end.

42

Be Aware of Yourself, Always

Let's put it this way: not being aware of yourself, allowing your thoughts to float, not knowing what you are thinking, not understanding your disposition within the contest of your position, not understanding how you are being perceived by others ... all of this allows a lazy complacency to set in, where creativity and innovation are stifled. But it goes beyond that, as your direction of things becomes stifled and stale also.

In most cases, one floats through the decision-making process—and life—on automatic pilot, unaware of the impact of the decisions one is making. Knowing what you are thinking, and understanding that you must have a constant awareness of yourself, forces your mind to constantly work. That does not mean you need to be aware of yourself putting food in your mouth at lunchtime. What it does mean is that you are aware of what you are doing as your subordinates are watching and are cognizant of your habits, manners, decision-making, vision, objectives, and goals. It's in your interest to be aware of yourself always so you know and understand your impact.

43

Regulate Your Emotional Impact

Have you ever heard someone say, "Control your emotions," or "Stop crying," or "Cheer up"? Easier said than done. As a leader or manager, your disposition is noticed and watched more than you know. Your every move, facial expression, and communication is under scrutiny ... not in a judgmental way, but as an innate and very natural process of subordinates assessing and balancing reaction and direction from you.

Something does not go as well as you thought it would, and one of your emotions kicks in. Whatever the circumstances, as soon as your team or staff notices, it will impact how they react to you and to other staff members.

As human beings, we find our emotions coming out quite naturally and unexpectedly at times, and yet we are pressured into keeping them subdued because of the very real and impactful repercussions. This goes to the awareness of yourself that you must have, understanding your value to and impact on others. If your emotions are obvious, they will affect others' behavior, and that's not good for any organization. Being emotional gives you a reputation for instability. A more stoic approach is always better in the work environment.

44

Set Productive Goals

So you have your goals. Now what? Once a goal is reached, the management and productivity of the goal are essential to its success. Is the goal having the effect you anticipated? Are there elements within that threaten its progress or continued success? The goal itself is just a point or benchmark reached. Its continued effect on additional goals requires maintaining or increasing productivity levels within that realm. If not, what may happen (and often does) is that the goal becomes a hollow victory with minimal return.

Whatever strategy was used to reach your goal was obviously the correct one. Therefore, the same effort, perseverance, and focus that was used to get there should be implemented to ensure the productive return of the effort. Otherwise, it was for naught. It's akin to reaching your goal of making a million dollars, and then two weeks later you wake up and have $998,000. What happened?

45

Control Your Disposition

Emotions impact judgment, depending on the strength of the emotion. Managing your emotions in a deliberate way and allowing your emotions to control you are two different things. Circumstances around you force out a subconscious memory of some kind or a previous experience, and an emotion like anger, sadness, or empathy will surface and may impact your judgment in an illogical way. Often the problem is not the emotion itself, but the lack of balance that the emotion creates. Emotions overwhelm the facts, blocking the brain's ability to logically work through an issue.

There is a way to correct this. It's called discipline of habit, and involves controlling your thoughts and knowing what you are thinking. If you don't do this, your brain will naturally think on its own with no clue about self-discipline. This is where managing your emotions comes in and allows you to take control of many areas of your leadership, focus, and objectives. Manipulating your thought process to discourage emotions and controlling your thoughts to the point of understanding what's happening around you will disallow the emotional disposition that holds you back.

46

Leverage Your Employees

Your employees all have their own strengths and weaknesses. By understanding their interests, knowing what they've been educated in, and assessing their work experience, you can get a good idea as to where they can or should be placed within the organization and the best project for them, hence for the organization.

The obvious benefit to this is morale. It's an age-old saying: if you like what you do, you'll be more conscientious and give it 110 percent. However, outside that benefit, the idea is to leverage your employees in a way that gives your team, department, and organization the benefit of targeted talent. By utilizing your human resources, you are able to balance and hedge your strategy for optimal results.

A lot of this sounds general, yes, and that's because there are many variables, talents, and circumstances with which to maneuver. Leveraging is applying a counterweight to offset a position where the outcome is unclear. By knowing your human resources, you give yourself an advantage for success in many ways.

47

Resolve Conflicts

Interoffice conflicts arise—it's inevitable. What's most important is that there is a way to work through the conflicts. Resolutions do not just arise; it takes a certain effort to accommodate ideas and work through them in a way that keeps productivity flowing.

Conflicts are a healthy part of any organization and are actually a sign of conscientious employees trying to make a difference. The trick is, how do you encourage these ideas beyond the conflict that they bring? An employee brought up the idea and conflict with another in the first place, so there should be a procedure in place to accommodate the conflict while not discouraging either idea.

Conflicts also exist with regard to client contracts, vendor contracts, internal policies contradicting customer relations, and so on. Your employees want to be involved in the resolution, which is good for morale. But outside the morale part of the equation is the simple fact that you do not have a monopoly on ideas. (Or you shouldn't, anyway.) If any conflict has a better resolution outcome, it will come from the employees who are involved. Their input is critical.

Conflict + Ideas + Employees = Resolution.

48

Monitor Relationships at Work

No, I'm not talking about the drama of the water cooler and who gives who the googly-eyes. Relationships at work refer to communication between pertinent employees within the context of a project or overall direction. It may sound trivial, but get a few employees who don't mix or some cliques forming and watch poor productivity and sabotage begin.

Again, this goes to knowing your employees and creating an atmosphere of cooperation and productivity. Your efforts do not need to be obvious in manipulating the environment to prevent such cliques and or personality conflicts that can sabotage progress. Stay involved, but, don't micromanage. The traps and vulnerabilities can be missed easily, but if you have your employees focused on the right things and in the right areas, you can nip problems in the bud.

Monitoring relationships at work in a subtle way is part of your job as an owner, manager, or project leader.

49

Know Your Workplace Culture

Workplace culture is probably the biggest factor in your success or failure. This can be broken down into three parts: creating a productive culture from the beginning, changing an unproductive culture, and functioning within an unproductive culture

First and foremost, your strategic plan must be understandable to the people who are going to be helping you implement it. You can't manage it alone, so that's important. Here is where the culture will be formulated. Your ability to set the tone of the organization will depend on:

- *How you train people to your vision.* Right from the get-go, your new hires should know what your vision is. Trust me, if they don't know your vision, they will be doing their own thing—and even if they know your vision, there must be constant strategic goals and benchmarks. Within the context of your vision is how the employees need to work through issues. Setting the tone creates a culture.

- *How you communicate issues and tasks.* No one likes meetings when they drag on and seem to produce nothing except more questions and wasted time. But meetings are necessary, and when run productively, they produce productive results—and an organizational culture that understands the seriousness of business. As a leader, you need to figure out how and what works best with the talent you have. Communicating effectively is part of the organization's culture.

- *How you organize responsibilities and accountabilities.* Balance the needs of the organization or department, distribute responsibilities to the proper talent, and then hold that talent accountable. The key word here is *balance.* Lack of balance alone can produce a culture of inefficiency that is very difficult to recover from. (This is why turnaround experts are needed.) Organizations lose their way. Having the right policies and procedures in place—and the right people handling them with deliberate progress and an understanding of the vision—produces a successful, productive, and efficient culture.

- *How you lead and the perception you give of your leadership.* If you are not respected, that becomes the culture. That's it. If you do not know how to lead, allow someone else to do it. If you allow mediocre results, that's your culture. How you lead and the perception your staff has of you will dictate their performance and trickle down to every aspect of the organization. You are being watched

> for verbal etiquette, fashion, seriousness, tolerance, facial expressions, emotions, understanding of tasks, delegating, self-control, attitude ... and the list goes on. That's what happens when you're a leader. Perceptions lead to judgments, to respect or disrespect, to a determination of the effectiveness of your leadership skills, and finally to a culture of decent or low productivity.

There are many books written about cultures within organizations. The vast majority are like textbooks that no one can actually follow. Why? Because a culture is based not on theories but on your disposition, knowledge, vision, character, determination, experience, morale-building, and the way all these factors are implemented and managed.

50

Build Competitive Teams

A sure way to build a competitive team or staff is to build trust first. Show your employees the context in which their decisions matter. You, as the leader, should be able to communicate the vision, flexibility, and versatility of the organization's or department's strategic plan. Your guidance in creating efficient procedures—in a way that's simple for everyone to understand—should allow for a clear direction and therefore a competitive team.

On the other hand, a sloppy approach that creates more disarray and a more reactionary method is a sure way to demoralize the team and build an uncompetitive culture. There's nothing worse than playing catch-up. It's one thing to be number two but still competitive if it's by design. But if it's simply a lack of leadership and strategy, well, watch your talent jump ship or worse, be unhappy in their position and mediocre in their performance. Trust me, once that sets in, the organization or department has set itself up for self-sabotage.

Building a competitive or uncompetitive team starts with the leadership and the implementation of a clear strategy.

51

Practice Effective Talent Management

Out of everything written in this book, this is probably the most important, because nothing will work without it. This is such a broad area because talent comes in all forms. Someone can be an absolute zero when it comes to numbers but a strategic genius. Someone can be a great orator but an absolute zero when it comes to organizing. And by the way, this includes yourself. (This is where knowing yourself comes into play.)

Honestly, the interview process is useless in determining talent. What happens if the interviewer does not phrase the questions properly to obtain a competent or relevant answer? That's unfair to the interviewee, and worse, it may botch the whole process. You may lose out on someone who was otherwise qualified. That's just one example, but the more important question is, how do you obtain and retain talent? Just like project management and crisis management, there is talent management. You need to find the right process, the right person within your organization to identify the proper talent, the right recruiting pool, the right criteria.

52

Don't Look Down on Lateral Moves

Many career advisors will tell you that if you're going to make a move within your company or even outside, make sure it's up. But before you swear off lateral moves, consider that they can be useful career-builders, as they broaden your skills and areas of expertise. In fact, some companies require their high-potentials to make several switches between functional tracks and general management before receiving a promotion. Next time you want to make a move, don't be distracted by a better title. Focus on your long-term career goals and consider the skills you need to get there. A lateral move may be the résumé enhancer you need.

53

Find Multiple Mentors

When people think of mentoring, they often think of a one-on-one relationship between a more experienced executive and someone still working his or her way through the politics and maze of the business world. But mentoring, like the rest of the work world, has changed over the past few decades.

Having that one person still works, but you can also try assembling a personal board of directors—a few people you know with experience and wisdom—who can advise you and help you work through issues. Mentoring is both a long-term and short-term arrangement. Nurture relationships with people whose perspective you respect so that you have a diverse (they do not have to be in your industry) group of people to speak with.

54

Cultivate Talent

The most successful businesses often thrive because of their talent. Getting the best people should be at the top of every manager's to-do list. But how?

Get to know talent before you need it. Spend time knowing your industry and department. Look around and know who's on your staff. Figure out who's performing, who are the potentials, the shining stars, what excites or motivates them about their work. Fostering and understanding these relationships early will pay off later. It's called *succession strategic preparedness*.

The most talented people get excited about working with leaders they can trust and learn from. Be sure people know why they should want to work for you. Do you have vision? Do you know what your boss's vision is?

Take time to cultivate promising individuals. The best talent is likely busy with other projects. Think of recruiting these people as part of a long-term game plan, regularly updating them about your vision for the future. Teach them and get them involved.

55

Become an Entrepreneur

It's a tough economy, but did you know what positive thing happens in recessions? People start their own businesses. It takes a lot of courage to do so. Do you have any ideas? The risks of entrepreneurship are many, but for those who are successful, the benefits are plentiful. It's hard work, but when you're successful, it's like hitting the lottery. The cash flow, well, *flows*. Here are some things to ask yourself before starting a business:

- *Do I have an idea?* It can't just be any idea. It has to be something you like and feel passionate about—something no one can talk you out of (because believe me, they will try).

- *Is there someone I trust?* Starting a business can be lonely. Doing it with someone else, especially someone with complementary skills, can make the road smoother and more fun. It also spreads the risk.

- *Do I perform best without structure?* For many, this is the biggest challenge. Everyone is different. If you thrive when there is no clear path and lots of uncertainty, it may be time to foster your inner entrepreneur, that inner rebel.

There's an ownership mentality that you should take in when conducting yourself in business. Asking yourself the right questions, such as; what can I do to make this project or task run more efficiently? Where can I innovate? How do I inspire and motivate others? What are the financial implications of doing it this way? Practicing this will increase your performance.

56

Rebel Now and Then

In our American culture, we like underdogs, entrepreneurs, and anyone who challenges the status quo. Yet many workplaces stifle creativity for not very good reasons—usually fear or defensiveness. Conformity and the status quo are comforting, and it's human nature to want to be comfortable. However, the result is usually a bland and unchallenging workplace. Challenging voices can help an organization, company, or department discover hidden talents, identify potential missteps, and engage in innovative thinking.

Honestly, you can rarely be an effective leader without having a little bit of rebel in you. Next time you find yourself agreeing with everyone in the room, ask yourself whether that's truly what's best for the property or your department. Play devil's advocate to test assumptions and poke holes in the strategy. Don't go too far, of course—you don't want to be a rebel without a cause. Knowing when to step back is just as important as knowing when to push.

57

Be Realistic About Assignments

Trying to accomplish a high-profile assignment—or even a normal one—in a short timeframe is often challenging. Taking on tough assignments (or ones perceived as tough) can cause some anxiety and often lead to failure or worse: you learn nothing from it and nothing gets done. That won't exactly help you or give you the experience you need in this competitive world.

Next time your manager recruits you for an assignment or project, seek out help if necessary. Ask for a few days to think it over. Don't be like a deer stuck in the headlights and do nothing, with an excuse only you understand. Don't pass it off, wait, and blame another for the delay.

Use your time to plan, identify the resources you'll need, and predict bottlenecks. Be realistic about what you can do and how to get it done. Then share what you've learned with your boss. Explain what you won't be able to do as a result of working on this assignment or project, and negotiate for the extra resources you'll need.

58

Don't Forget the Follow-Up

One of the biggest mistakes people make after receiving a favor or referral is failing to follow up. Not good—in many cases you may look ungrateful, or worse, like you just have bad manners or etiquette. Whether someone gives you advice on a job application or makes an introduction to a colleague or client, be sure to give that person some feedback as to what happened or didn't happen.

It's simply the right thing to do. It's closing a loop that can be of help in the future. That person may be able to help further by making another introduction or suggesting or another place to apply. Never burn a bridge.

59

Be Careful When Giving References

Dismissing an employee is a stressful and challenging task. No one likes it. Unfortunately, the difficulties don't always end when the individual is out the door. Employees, even those you let go, may ask you for references. Be careful and:

- *Verify information.* Check the former employee's file before giving a reference to ensure that you state just the facts. Do not deviate from the facts.
- *Keep it short.* Whether you're writing a reference letter or providing a phone reference, limit the amount of information you offer. Remember, surrender very little. This will reduce your chances of saying anything that could be perceived as defamatory.
- *Keep it factual.* Again, limit your responses to factual information only—dates of employment, title, salary, and other objective data.

60

Start Your Day Right

When you're working on large goals—or any goals, for that matter—days can easily blend together. Instead of thinking about what needs to happen today, you're focusing on what needs to get done this week, this month, this quarter. It's natural; it's what people do. But try not to lose sight of what's in front of you: one day of work. If you're focused on the task, and you commit to doing something that day, you are essentially building brick by brick. Many opportunities, decisions, and additional issues may arise, but the important thing is that there is momentum. Remember the phrase, "If you're standing still, you're going backward." Not good.

By starting each day right, you're more likely to do the work that leads to achievement of those bigger goals. When you begin your day, pause and ask yourself whether you are ready for what is to come. It's called contemplating—or if you want, meditating. That doesn't mean you grab an orange and start humming to it; it just means slow down and think through things before your day starts. Are you prepared for all your meetings? Do you know what work you need to accomplish? What risks can you anticipate and prepare for? Answering these questions will help you make the most of each day and set you up for success in the long term.

61

Encourage Risk-Taking

Over the past few years, the economy has taken a hit and forced many businesses to play it safe and buckle down. I speak about corporate culture quite a bit, and it's time for you to assess your responsibility in holding on to it or changing it. What has your department or sphere of influence become? Has it always been this way, so you bear no responsibility in changing it? Are you afraid to take risk? Maybe it's time for a 180. Here's how to start:

- *Evaluate risk-taking.* Take an honest look at your department and consider whether people avoid risks. Are you instilling that in them? Utilize interviews or one-on-one meetings to assess which of your staff is risk-adverse or ambitious. Include yourself.

- *Make idea-sharing comfortable.* Create a safe

space where managers and employees can voice their concerns, feedback, and ideas without fear of retribution. It's not 1970 anymore ... "command and control" is dead. Do not suppress your staff or managers.

- *Experiment.* Ask employees and managers to do tasks that you do. Allow cycle experiments to test new ways of working. Make it explicit that failure is acceptable as long as learning comes from it.

There's a time to play it safe, and there's a time not to. Now is the time "not to." Too many companies with smart people are around us making decisions that will impact our sales and revenue. Understand the culture and how you've assimilated into it—positively or negatively. Balance the changes necessary while preserving the attributes and qualities that make it work. That's managing!

62

Plan for Promotions

Promotions are a useful tool for recognizing and motivating top employees. Next time you consider moving someone to the next level, do these things first:

- *Assess current performance.* Be sure the employee can do the job you might promote him or her into. Take a look at the employee's current performance and look for things that may indicate future performance. Making allowances is not always a good idea.

- *Make sure there is a match.* Consider whether the new position is something the employee will enjoy doing. Just because someone is good at a job doesn't mean he or she will take pleasure in it, and a problem with performance can arise quickly. Oops!

- *Experiment before pulling the trigger.* Design an assignment that is similar to the tasks and challenges of the new job to test the employee's ability.

Now, these are somewhat simplistic, but they're a start. Vetting and focusing seriously on the candidate is critical. Think about it like this: if you can't fit this individual into your vision or long-term strategy for your department or organization in a way that gives you little doubt, then stop. It's way easier to plop someone into an important position than it is to reassess.

63

Keep Troublemakers On Task

It can be incredibly frustrating when a colleague seems to agree with a plan of action or pretends to be on the same page, only to go off and do his or her own thing (whether deliberately or not). This is sabotage, and it is all too common, making it difficult to achieve your goals or the goals of the organization as a whole. Try these solutions:

- *Give feedback.* Explain to your colleague what you're seeing and experiencing. Describe the impact of the behavior on you and your efforts, and provide suggestions for how it might change.

- *Focus on work, not the person.* You need to get the work done despite your peer's style, so don't waste time wishing he or she would change. Concentrate on completing the work instead. The momentum will keep things moving forward. Remember what

I've told you in the past: if you can't change the person (and chances are you can't), then change the environment.

- *Ask for commitment.* At the end of a meeting, have every employee (not just the difficult one) reiterate what he or she is going to do and by when. Sometimes peer pressure can keep even the most passive-aggressive blocker on task.

The bigger point here is that we are all working toward the same goal as one—or we should be. Understanding and changing others (or yourself) is not easy, but it is imperative. It takes forward thinking, it takes reassessing, it takes the absolute thought process of, "Wait a minute, am I blocking something or sabotaging something for a reason?" or "Am I doing something a certain way that's not getting the results we need?"

64

Give Your Boss Bad News

No one likes to deliver bad news. But sitting on problems rather than putting them out in the open only makes things worse. Next time you have to tell your boss that something has gone wrong, try these tactics:

- *Describe.* Provide a general overview of the problem and explain the impact. Be sure to position this in terms of what matters to your boss. Don't be long-winded about it—a big explanation is not necessary and wastes time. "Just the facts, ma'am!"

- *Identify a solution.* Recommend a specific solution or approach, along with alternatives. You should always have a solution or solutions.

- *Analyze your solution.* Share the pros and cons

and explain the implications. Be prepared to discuss the risks or barriers that may be of concern to your boss. It is your job and responsibility to think through problems and issues.

- *Accept responsibility.* Let your boss know that you are willing to take the responsibility for the outcome of your proposed approach.

65

Ask for Compromises and Favors

Asking someone for a big favor or help can be daunting. But you should not be embarrassed or shy about doing it. It implies a humbling, and that is good. Follow these steps:

1. *Set it up.* Think through the reasons first and then be explicit about the nature of your favor or request. Be ready to compromise. The phrase "I have a favor to ask" implies a contract in which you will someday try to return the favor.
2. *Explain.* People like to know why they are being asked to do something. "Can you cover that meeting for me?" is far less effective than "Can you cover that meeting for me because I have another meeting I can't miss?"

3. *Give an out.* No one feels good about being forced to do something. Offer an escape route by saying, "If you can't, I understand," or "I know you're busy."

I understand this sounds simplistic, but it's these soft necessities that reduce resistance between us. It's productive.

66

Gain Good Judgment

Reversing a decision that isn't working out can be a painful experience. The traditional thought in business is to be decisive and have an unwavering adherence to your decisions. But perhaps the policy you changed or implemented isn't working, or a position you've taken on something and were behind is falling flat. Whatever the issue, accepting failure and changing direction can feel like a comment on your judgment.

In these situations, it's not a bad idea to call on others to help you evaluate and redirect. A variety of perspectives can help—there's nothing wrong with finding out what went wrong and adjusting. Reversing a decision shouldn't be a reason for shame. Remember the saying, "We learn from our mistakes." Those are not empty words. They came from someplace.

That's not to say you can make continual errors and think it's okay because you are learning—that would be unproductive. But your judgment is important; it is gained by your experience. Assess and strategize when making decisions.

67

Respect Your Boss and Colleagues

This is more about professionalism than anything else. The way we treat each other in the workplace is the way our customers get treated. If you do not communicate with your boss and colleagues effectively, then that is extended to your customers. If you are not cooperating with your boss or colleagues, then that is extended to your customers.

In other words, your actions, attitude, and reactions are all connected and extended in some way. It's organization, it's efficiency, it's creativity, it's thinking, it's streamlining.

When you communicate with a customer, you likely have on your "game face" and project a high degree of professionalism. Do you do the same with colleagues? Subordinates? Whether you are talking with your assistant manager, your supervisors, your boss, your subordinates, or a customer, it pays to be thoughtful and articulate every time. When you ask a question, make sure it's a smart one. When you present an analysis or have an idea, spend a few minutes thinking ahead about your key message, supporting details, and follow-up. This shows your staff how it's done—that you have respect for them. It also shows those paying attention that you are smart and competent.

I don't want there to be a mixed message here. It's okay to make light of things sometimes; it's okay to not be professional in certain circumstances; it's okay that your boss, colleagues, and staff know that you are human. We should all be comfortable and confident with our shared direction. It's a balance that you need to achieve. That's what leadership is.

(By the way, this is not a "Can't we all just get along" moment. Internal competition is healthy in any organization.)

68

Know Who You Are

What drives some companies to succeed while others languish? For example, why does Kmart struggle while Walmart and Target thrive? What the former lacks that the latter two have nailed is a coherent and distinctive "way to play." The same can be said for any business.

Walmart focuses on low prices and a welcoming atmosphere. Target caters to a similarly cost-conscious customer set but focuses more on image and design. Which one are you? Have you made it clear? Is your vision clear to you? We can't be all things to all people, so our decisions need to be in the context of providing differentiated value for a specific set of customers. This means deciding what we won't provide and what we will. The focus that comes from this vision is important. It's important that you work your department, staff, projects, and tasks to that end.

As competition increases around us, there is no time to lose or squander. You know what you have to do.

69

Don't Worry

A certain amount of anxiety is an inevitable part of our lives, but in today's fast-paced world, it can become overwhelming. Too much stress hinders productivity and can be dangerous to your health. Here are some things you can do to keep anxiety from becoming toxic:

- *Talk to someone you trust.* This can be a friend, a partner, or a colleague. Sometimes just talking can be a relief—it's called venting—and your listener may provide some reassuring guidance.

- *Get the facts.* Often a small problem can get blown out of proportion. Do not allow the situation to become embellished; it's no good for anyone. Before you let worry consume you, get the facts. Find out what, and how big, the real problem is.

- *Let it go.* When you can't do anything about the problem, give it up and forget about it. This may be easier said than done, but it is worth the conscious effort.

There's an ancient Indian (Hindu) proverb that may put things into perspective. It's called, "Don't Worry":

> If you are worried about something, and you have control,
>
> *don't worry*—fix it.
>
> If you are worried about something, and you have no control over it,
>
> *don't worry*—there's nothing you can do.

70

Expand and Sharpen Your Skills to Stay Relevant

The world of work changes quickly. The skills that make you successful today probably won't be the same tomorrow. This means that whatever your specialty, it's at risk of being outdated soon. You don't need a crystal ball to see what skills you'll need in the future. Instead, actively seek out opportunities that allow you to develop new skills, gain different experiences, and expand your networks and knowledge. Doing this will create more alternatives and options in your future. Don't forget to think about what value these new skills bring to your organization and your department. Being valuable is another way to expand your future options.

Do not relax, do not become complacent, do not believe the current is forever—and remember that no one is indispensable. Build your knowledge and experience and work through the issues that can help you by tapping and sharpening your skills every day.

71

Bring Out the Best in Your Boss

How can you help with tasks and projects—the overall vision? While you can't change your boss, you may be able to alter the dynamic of your relationship. Focus on trying to better utilize him or her by doing the following:

- *Exploit your boss's strengths.* Figure out what your boss excels at and tap into those skills when they are most useful. For example, if he is good at big-picture thinking, ask him to share his vision for driving your critical project forward. Then focus on his vision for your project or task.

- *Listen to learn.* Many bosses are critical of ideas that they haven't generated. Next time your boss talks down your idea, listen. While it may be hard to hear, his critique could include useful feedback that improves your proposal.

The important thing here is to utilize and move forward ideas that are within the vision. Do not get stuck; do not get distracted or derailed by focusing on other projects or departments. Fix your house first, and when you all focus on this, you can suggest and recommend other tasks outside your department with a vision of benefiting the organization as a whole.

72

Maintain Your Composure

Most people have moments at work that make them upset or bring them to tears: a colleague gets laid off, your idea is criticized, you receive a particularly bad performance review. No one is immune to hurt feelings. Next time you're having a bad day and feel like shedding a tear at work, here's what you can do instead:

1. *Get out of the office.* Excuse yourself politely and then head to the nearest bathroom or coffee shop, call a friend or family member and vent, or simply take a walk outside for fresh air. The idea is to separate yourself from the situation to release your emotions, and then reassess.
2. *Revisit the situation.* Once you've had a chance to calm down, take another look at the problem. If you were wronged, speak with your colleague

or boss in private and look for some explanation or feedback. Maintain your composure and offer suggestions on solutions.

73

React Appropriately to a Crisis

The way a company deals with disruptions speaks volumes about management. Responding effectively can often be the difference between an interruption and a disaster. Next time you are faced with a crisis, do the following:

- *Figure out what happened.* Too many people or leaders leap into action without assessing the situation first. Find out exactly what is going on and what's causing it.

- *Act promptly.* Don't wait for all of the data to come in. Once you have a firm grasp of the situation, begin taking action. Don't act frazzled—that only worries people. Act with deliberateness and speed.

- *Adapt.* Don't be wedded to a single strategy.

Circumstances will change, and new information will come to light. Be prepared to alter your course if necessary. Remember, the best battle plans go astray: you need to adapt to the change in circumstances.

74

Think

When working on a challenging task, creating new policies and procedures, or looking at your own productivity, it's helpful to get feedback from others. Do they think it's any good? In what direction do they think you should take it?

Sometimes, though, too much feedback can drown out the most important opinion of all: your own. If you feel like you're getting too much input or are no longer sure what you think of your own direction, take a break from the feedback. Think. Contemplate. This will build your confidence and trust in yourself. Once you've articulated and refined your own perspective, reach back out to others.

75

Establish Rituals

Many people constantly feel starved for time; they hurry through the day while fighting countless distractions and struggling to stay focused. A way to remain calm and centered is by bringing rituals into your workday. Rituals are about paying attention—they help you "set up." If you take a moment to notice what you are about to do, you remind yourself to appreciate and focus on the task rather than rush through it. For example, when you sit down at your desk in the morning, pause. Take a deep breath and give thought to what you are about to do. You may find this focus helps you accomplish tasks more carefully and productively.

76

Give Up Your Protective Mindset

In the Middle Ages, in an effort to protect and further the skills and knowledge of their members—their area of control—tradesmen would form guilds, "us against them." For example, blacksmiths might band together to defend trade secrets and corner markets. Unfortunately, this mentality is still alive and well between many organizations and also internally, within the organizations themselves. You can call them silos, cells, clicks, whatever ... internal organizational functions have their areas of special expertise and at times expend energy trying to guard it from others. Competition between functions or departments can be healthy, but not if it leads to unproductive jousting. Focus that competition on external forces, not internal ones. Departments should work together to become a team of specialists that spans or transcends hoarding.

77

Produce Results, Don't Just Talk About Them

Talk, thoughts, recommendations, suggestions, and planning are all nice, but are nothing without implementation. They produce *no* actual results.

Try focusing on making changes, not just proposing them. The first step is to alter the nature of the task. Don't ask around to "look at" or "study" a certain issue. Challenge yourself to solve it: set benchmarks for yourself, look to improve the speed of a process, experiment if necessary. Encourage yourself and your staff to try possible, different improvements to see which works. Not all will, of course, but you will build momentum for implementation and prepare the department, thereby organizing for change. (Remember, change is good.) You may still want to look into and study somewhat, but it should cover what's been done, not what can be done.

78

Focus on Your Capabilities and Responsibilities

Instead of looking for strategies in other places, outperform competitors by leveraging what the company does best. Use the company's capabilities—the people, knowledge, systems, tools, and processes that create value for customers—as the foundation of competitive advantage. Here are some ways to make this work:

- *Put capabilities first.* Don't decide on a strategic direction and then wonder what you need to get there. Look at your core strengths, and let those drive your strategy.
- *Identify differentiating capabilities.* Figure out what the company does uniquely well, what your customers value, and what your competitors can't emulate.

- *Focus on capabilities, not just fixed assets.* Fixed assets tend to expire or become obsolete. Capabilities help keep you agile because they can be applied to changing circumstances. Try to put this into context from your recent reviews.

79

Interview, Again

Most managers feel more invested in people they've hired personally. They've reviewed the résumés, conducted the interviews, and made the ultimate decision. While in your existing job, consider getting "hired" all over again by doing some simple things:

- *Update your résumé.* This may be, in the traditional sense, for your own benefit. In any format, focus on your recent accomplishments.

- *Set up a meeting.* Ask for an appointment with your boss. Get an idea of his or her priorities. Treat this like an interview—be on time and act professionally.

- *Present yourself.* Start by saying, "Let me tell you about my role and what I believe to be our goal." Review and think about your résumé, your presentation, and how you present yourself to colleagues and clients. Highlight your achievements and those of your department.. Find out what you can about your boss's interests, needs, and vision.

Ask yourself, "Am I achieving my goals? Am I helping to achieve the goals of the organization, or am I floating along?"

80

Know When Not to Delegate

Most management experts will advise you to delegate as much as possible. This is because delegating develops your employees and gives you time to focus on the bigger picture. Yet there are times when delegating may not be so prudent or right, such as:

- *When there's lack of clarity.* If you can't explain precisely the problem that needs solving or how best to do it, hold off. Wait until you have greater insight to share.

- *When you need the learning.* It's good to develop others, but don't sacrifice your own development. Hold on to tasks that contribute significantly to your own growth.

- *When the project is too high-stakes.* There are

times when you are truly the best person for the job—not because you will get it done faster or better, but because the project is too important to pass on to others.

Note: Taking into context all of these reasons, this is not an excuse to "sit" on something. Speed is still of the essence. There are many projects your company is working on now that need to be pushed through. You know what they are. Chop, chop!

81

Get Your Ideas Through

When you have an idea, don't assume that others will share your enthusiasm for it. Whether a recommendation or proposal is approved often depends on how it is presented. Here are a few things you can do to give your idea a chance:

- *Build allies.* Meet with others before you implement or pitch your idea in order to generate interest.

- *Keep it simple.* Don't weigh your proposal down with tons of data, analysis, and talk. Too many details are distracting. Be straightforward and concise.

- *Highlight the benefits.* How can it work? Be sure to position the idea in terms of the benefits.

82

Get Unstuck

There are times of the year, or the week, or the day when you simply have too much to do. You may buckle down and focus—or, like many people, you may get overwhelmed and freeze up. Next time you are stressed out by how much you need to accomplish, follow these steps:

1. *Make a list.* Write down everything you need to do on a piece of paper. It sounds trivial or simple, but it helps.
2. *Do the quick hits.* Take fifteen minutes, no more, to do the fastest things on your list—a quick e-mail response, a two-minute phone call. Stay focused on the timing and task.

3. *Turn off distractions.* Now spend thirty-five minutes focused on the tougher things. Get help when you need it.

4. *Take a break and repeat.* Take a ten-minute break and start again. Before long, you'll have crossed enough off your list to restore your calm and productivity.

83

Speak Effectively

Successfully communicating with your customers is the foundation for how you are perceived in their eyes and how you gain their repeat business. Listed below are a few tactics that may increase the likelihood that your customers hear what you are saying:

- *Understand their language.* This does not mean you need to learn Portuguese, Swahili, or Mongolian. It means your approach should be to listen not just to *what* people are saying but *how* they are saying it. One-size-fits-all sales or customer-service pitches do not always work and can actually sound robotic. The reality is that our customers speak a unique language informed by their life experiences. Tailor your approach and your language for each customer.

- *Focus on them, not you.* It's tempting when trying to solve a problem to talk about "the company." Instead, turn the spotlight on your customers. Talk about their problems, their needs, and their plans.

84

Accept Temporary Solutions

When looking to make a change, reorganize your department, a policy, or develop a new system, people often seek out solutions that will last as long as possible. They want them to be sustainable, after all. But nothing lasts forever. A permanent solution may not be feasible, or may even be a miscalculation. Next time you need to make a big change, come up with a temporary solution, if necessary—not a final one. Most approaches are useful for a certain amount of time. When that time's over, you need a new way to attack the problem, since it's likely to morph.

85

Control the Customer Experience

Whether you're aware of it or not, every interaction we have with our customers contributes to their larger experience with the company. Perhaps you are aware of this in some form and carefully and thoughtfully look to micromanage the experience in hopes of influencing positive comments. It has to be more natural than that. Despite calculated efforts, customers will not always perceive us as we wish. People don't behave or react exactly how you expect they will, but don't give up because of this unpredictability. Accept it as part of the challenge and frequently monitor what customers are experiencing. By getting their input and feedback, and observing them in real time, you can adjust your efforts accordingly. Perfect control is not necessary to influence their opinions. Continue to aim for the ideal and make modifications as needed. That's management!

86

Find the Most Meaningful Metrics

Many people find it easy to identify metrics or standards that measure the worth of their work—salespeople have sales targets, for example, and department heads track budgets and productivity levels. But not all jobs or skills are so easily quantifiable, and far too many people choose not to measure at all. If you fall into this category, invent a new, innovative metric that gets at the real value of what you do. For example, if one of your critical roles is to develop your people, rather than looking at how many training opportunities you provide for your staff or team, focus on an outcome measurement, such as how many people you effectively brokered into successful performance within the organization. Or count the number of ideas generated by your staff or yourself, and how many of those went on to become valuable policies or procedures with a tangible impact on the bottom line.

87

Avoid the Two Pitfalls of Past Practices

When embarking on a new project or trying to upgrade a process, it can be invaluable to know the way things have been done in the past. Yet when it comes time to implement changes, these same past practices are useless. Because they can't let go of the old comfortable way of doing things, many organizations fall short in competing. Next time you want to do what the best in the industry is doing, avoid these two hazards:

1. *Failure to adapt.* What worked in one company for many years will not likely work in a new competitive environment. Look to customize your product and service, retrain staff, and assess your culture, environment, and people. Tailor any lesson from others to fit your unique situation.

2. *Failure to adopt.* A borrowed process or tool won't work unless you have commitment from leadership and those responsible for using it. Be sure you have full support before you implement.

88

Don't Dismiss the Importance of Service and Product

There are many misconceptions about value when it comes to products and services. Unfortunately, these widely held beliefs often keep managers, leaders, and owners from realizing the potential of good product and service. Here are a few common misconceptions that may be holding you back:

- *A once-successful strategy is more important than improving the actual product or service.* Strategy is critical—there is no arguing that. But evolving the product and enhancing the service are also critical in competing. In fact, customers notice the effort more than you know.

- *Customers care more about price.* That may be

true, but it doesn't have to be an either-or decision where service especially is sacrificed. A great product with an attention to detailed service that complements the product can work with a well-thought-out price point.

89

Give Your Employees the Direction They Need

All too often, people work hard on a project without fully understanding the organization's overall goals. Next time your staff isn't sure where it's headed, think about these points:

- *Don't assume everyone knows the strategy.* It's a mistake to believe that just because executives have shared the strategy, your people understand it.

- *Confirm shared understanding.* Sketch out a from-to chart that shows where your organization is now and where it is headed. Share this with your boss and your team to be sure you are all on the same page.

- *Connect the dots.* Create two lists—one of the major projects and one of the organization's goals. Draw lines between the two lists. If there are projects that don't line up, consider refocusing or killing them.

90

Turn Around Your Performance

No one likes to be an underperformer. Yet failing to meet expectations doesn't have to feel like the end of the world. Follow these steps to help turn your poor performance around:

- *Accept it and ask for help.* Don't be defensive. If the subtle and sometimes not-so-subtle feedback and data show you are underperforming, accept it and ask for help to get better. Ask others—especially your boss—to share insights about how you can improve.

- *Understand the underlying cause.* Do you not have the right skills? Are you uninterested in the work? Whatever it is, get to the bottom of what's causing you to come up short. Many times complacency sets in, and an idea that "I deserve better" will subconsciously affect your performance, which in turn has an impact on subordinates and colleagues.

- *Feeling staid.* You may believe that a minimal performance level is all that's needed; however, this will not stimulate your creativity and overall work ethic. I promise, the competition is fierce out there. Your performance counts.
- *Commit to change.* Identify what it is you need to do differently, and ask those around you to keep you accountable. Smart people surround themselves with smart people.

91

Have Those Tough Conversations

It's often difficult to have conversations about sensitive subjects. Whether you need to tell someone you disagree with her approach or are upset by his behavior, it's all too easy to put it off in hopes of finding the "perfect time." Chances are, that time will never come. You'll be better off if you stop procrastinating and make the conversation happen.

Request a time to meet. Use a nonthreatening medium, such as e-mail or voicemail, to ask what time would be best to discuss a sensitive matter. You'll likely still worry before you sit down with the person, but by framing the conversation upfront, you'll have taken some of the charge out of it.

92

Get Rid of the Negativity

Every organization, unit, or team has both good and bad. As a boss, is it your job to accentuate the positive or eliminate the negative? You should try to do both, but studies have shown that negative information, experiences, and people have a far deeper impact than positive ones. It is a better use of your time and energy to focus on clearing your organization of the negatives as much as you can. This may mean tearing down frustrating obstacles or shielding people from destructive behavior. Grumpiness, laziness, and nastiness are contagious, and by reducing those types of negativity, you give your people a better chance to shine.

93

Cut Down on Organizational Clutter

There's nothing like moving offices to force you to de-clutter; it gives you the impetus to purge materials you've been holding on to for years "in case I need them." It's called useless clutter. Also, there are intangible things like processes, procedures, rules, and policies that have outlived their usefulness. You don't need to relocate your office to uncover the drive to de-clutter. Instead, think about where you want to go next and whether you can get there with the clutter you've accumulated. Clutter holds you back and creates unnecessary confusion and distracting thoughts. Frame a challenging goal, such as increasing customer face-time or understanding value and revenue. Ask yourself, "How do I streamline our processes to get there?"

94

Cultivate Your Proactive Mind

Studies have shown that a good memory helps you better navigate the future. And in business, the ability to anticipate and negotiate future demands is an asset. A proactive mind uses details from past experiences to make analogies with your current surroundings. It then helps you determine where you are and envision future possibilities. We are all born with proactive minds, but these things may help improve your brain performance:

- *Give your brain a lot to work with.* Create a richer pool of information to draw from. Expose your brain to diverse experiences and situations.

- *Borrow from others.* Find out as much as you can about others' experiences by talking, interacting with, and reading about them. Build on it. Learn from it.

- *Let your mind wander.* Undisturbed time gives your brain the space it needs to recall and recombine past experiences in ways that help you anticipate the future. Contemplation exercises your mind and helps you to strategize.

- *Know what you're thinking.* By not being aware of what you are thinking, your brain goes into auto mode and simply makes decisions and considers issues as a mundane process. By constantly knowing what you are thinking you take command of that process and assess in a much more fluid and controlled manner. It stimulates awareness, and with awareness comes understanding.

95

Motivate Employees Who Have Become Set in Their Ways

Employees who are slow to react can be frustrating, especially in environments where it's imperative to respond and adapt to change quickly. However, we should not always assume these slowpokes are trying to undermine progress or resist change. They may have very good reasons for their slow response times. So we may want to wait on someone's input, perhaps talk to him or her. Maybe explain that we are all under pressure and that you value knowing his or her response. Ask that person to get back to you quickly, within a day or so. He or she may have a thoughtful rationale for proceeding cautiously, and realizing that the matter is in his or her hands may speed things up.

Honestly, this is the patient route. Change is something that, at times, needs to be forced through. Remember what I've said in the past: if you cannot change the person, change the environment, and that person will conform.

96

Learn to Handle Criticism

Criticism is tough to take in any form. Unforeseen negative feedback can be unsettling but also incredibly valuable. Next time you are blindsided by what someone has to say about your behavior or performance, try to do the following:

- *Move beyond your feelings*. You're likely to feel hurt and angry. Notice those feelings, and then put them aside so they don't influence your reaction.
- *Look beyond the delivery*. Giving feedback is hard, and very few people are skilled at it. Don't dismiss the feedback just because it wasn't delivered well.
- *Collect the data*. Don't respond right away. You'll likely regret how defensive and angry you sound. Instead, listen. Take in the criticism. Once you've had time and space, you can decide how to react and whether to change.

97

Be Careful with One-Size-Fits-All Management

When the job market picks up, the first to leave are often a company's most valuable employees. Unfortunately, you may be inadvertently encouraging these future leaders to say their goodbyes by treating them as cogs in a wheel rather than the individuals they are. Instead of managing everyone the same way, know your employees.

- *Customize the position.* Not in a way that will disrupt operations or create dissension or envy, but by knowing what each employee's strengths, weaknesses, and preferences are. If your star performer doesn't want to manage people, don't make him or her do it. Don't put that individual on the spot.

- *Customize the rewards*. Employees want different things. A parent may want flextime, while an ambitious recent college grad may be looking for outside training or a mentor. Give people what they want, not what upper management has decided is best for them to have.

98

Explain Change

Setting a new direction, changing behavior, or transforming a culture is never easy. But it's doable when everyone involved has an understanding as to the reasons why it is necessary. Your employees will need certain things in order to achieve this.

- *A clear destination.* Many change efforts fail because not everyone understands where the company is headed. Be clear up front with everyone who needs to change about what the endpoint looks like. Not understanding this and accepting the status quo because it's easier undermines everyone else's efforts.

- *A starting point.* Big goals are intimidating and sometimes paralyzing. Get started by taking small steps toward your goal. Momentum will build. Create your own strategic plan to reach the goal and changes necessary.

- *Persistence.* Most change efforts look like they will fail at some point, usually in the middle. Don't give up prematurely. Find a way around obstacles, make necessary alterations, and keep going. We've discussed this point a number of times—maintaining the changes is critical. It's human nature to seek and retreat back into what's comfortable. Get on board and stay there.

99

Understand Your Review

Receiving a less-than-stellar performance review can be upsetting. It seems like a direct attack on your ego. How you handle it is far more important than the content of the review itself.

- *Think before reacting.* It's far too easy to be defensive. Let the results sink in before you do anything. Does the feedback ring true? Does it resonate with things you've heard in the past?

- *Decide what to change.* You don't have to respond to everything. Getting much better at one thing is far better than slightly improving on several fronts. Decide which feedback is most important to you as a leader and focus on that.

- *Ask for help or advice.* Once you've committed to

changing, ask your manager or colleague—someone you trust. Don't allow yourself to fall back into patterns that have not helped in the past.

100

Protect Your Good Idea

Even the best idea can die when naysayers raise concerns, even if the concerns are meritless. Instead of trying to dodge unavoidable attacks, learn to expect the common types you'll face and counter them simply and convincingly.

- *Death by delay:* Adversaries may try to put off the discussion, ask for additional information, or otherwise delay a decision on your idea, thereby slowing momentum. Keep your audience focused on making a decision.

- *Confusion:* Detractors often present distracting information or try to link your idea to several others in an attempt to confound people. Be clear about what your idea is and what it isn't.

- *Fear-mongering:* Nothing kills an idea faster

than irrational anxieties. Know what fears your challengers might stir up and be prepared to allay them.

101

Support Your People

There are countless distractions, threats, and roadblocks to getting work done. Good bosses take pride in shielding their people from these annoyances. Here are three ways you can help your employees focus on what matters:

1. *Show up on time.* One of the biggest detractors from work is wasted time. This might be time your people spend waiting for you to show up to meetings or to give needed direction. Being important doesn't give you permission to impede productivity.
2. *Stop the intrusions.* Set aside time when your employees can think and work, and not be expected to respond right away. In other words, minimize their distractions, help them focus, support them. This does not mean go out of your way to do nice things; it means helping them succeed in their position, from which the company will benefit too.

3. *Let them fight good fights.* Don't avoid conflict. Make your people feel safe enough to speak their minds—even to you—so they have productive and creative disagreements. This is important. Short of insubordination and dissension, it should be okay that they discuss things and speak up. That means they are thinking. Thinking is good. It helps you succeed.

102

Stop Being So Nice

Conflict avoidance is a common trait of many workplaces. But steering clear of disagreements and leaving things unsaid creates needless complexity and anxiety—and worse, paralysis of plans. Here are some ideas that may help you to be better at confronting conflict constructively:

- *Reflect.* Ask yourself whether there are times you should've spoken up but held your tongue. Do you avoid certain types of conflict?

- *Get feedback.* Ask trusted friends and colleagues how they perceive your readiness to engage in constructive conflict. They might see patterns that are less obvious to you. But, honestly, look within yourself. You know best.

- *Experiment.* You don't have to change overnight.

Try pushing back on a request or speaking up in a meeting and see how it goes. Practice and make it a habit. Our habits define us.

103

Refocus Your Team on a New Strategy

Most strategic change initiatives fail, or at least hit some major bumps along the road. If your team is struggling to adapt to a new strategy, try these three things to get back on track:

1. *Push decision-making downward.* If people are told to act differently, they feel like sheep, with little control or power. Let people make choices about how they will contribute to the new strategy.
2. *Ask for input.* If your people are stuck, ask them to suggest ways to remove the barriers that are holding them back.

3. *Share successes.* No one wants to change if they don't think the new strategy will succeed. Whenever you make progress, no matter how small, share it with your team as evidence that the new strategy is working.

104

Don't Be a Martyr-Boss

The best bosses shelter their people from disruption and stress. But you shouldn't put your employees' comfort or happiness ahead of the tasks that are necessary to the efficient operation of your department. Sacrificing yourself will only lead to burnout and resentment. This is especially true if you have weak or destructive people on your team. Whether you hired or inherited them, your job is to help them improve—and if they don't, to help them move on. Your position requires you to support your subordinates and help them grow. It's good for your department, it's good for business, and it's the right way to do things.

Don't be afraid to talk to a staff member if he or she is a weak link. It does you no favors, and certainly does the employee no favors, to keep him or her on a task or in a position where growth is impossible.

105

Help Your Organization Make Better Decisions

While individuals ultimately make decisions, organizations influence and shape the decision-making process. In fact, an organization can boost its employees' capacity for good judgment and improve the chances they will make good and sound decisions. Here are a few ways to make it happen:

- *Examine decisions made.* Upon completion of a project, ask your staff to discuss which things they would do again and which they wouldn't. By reflecting on the decisions that went into the project and their results, people can prepare to make better decisions the next time around.

- *Be okay with restarting.* When bad decisions

happen, don't make everyone suffer the consequences. Start the project over so that people can learn from their mistakes.

- *Give people autonomy.* People need space to make well-grounded decisions. When they are in control of the decisions and responsible for the consequences, they are more likely to exercise good judgment. It's called accountability.

106

Walk Away When You Need To

With offices becoming more physically and metaphorically open, the privacy of a room with a closed door can be difficult to find. More often, everyone from the CEO to the receptionist is visible to everyone else. This level of exposure encourages transparency but can also put you on display in fragile moments when you are stressed or upset. Next time you feel like you might lose your cool (and who hasn't had those moments?), take note of where you are. If you might be observed by others, take a deep breath or a drink of water. If that doesn't do the trick, get outside. In these new open workspaces, it's critical to maintain professionalism by being calm and supportive of others, and by doing your venting somewhere private.

107

Quietly Promote Change

A leader or manager who pushes a change agenda too hard risks building resistance and resentment, or even alienating his people. Here are some ways you can challenge the prevailing wisdom and make change happen ... quietly:

Model the change. Demonstrate the way you want things to change through your own language and behavior. Often, seeing a leader do something first gives people the courage to try it themselves.

Turn negatives into positives. Find ways to reframe people's resistance as an opportunity for change. This requires that you listen carefully, understand the underlying reasons for the opposition, and address them directly.

Find allies. Chances are someone else in the organization wants the change as badly as you do. Find that person and pool your resources and ideas.

108

Create a Simple Strategic Principle

Helping employees understand a strategy while simultaneously motivating them to achieve it is a huge challenge for many leaders. Creating and sticking to a pithy, memorable, action-oriented phrase can help. When designed and executed well, a strategic principle gives employees clear direction while inspiring them to be flexible and take risks. A powerful strategic principle forces trade-offs between competing resources and provides a litmus test for decisions. When faced with a choice, an employee should be able to test his or her options against the strategic principle to make a decision that aligns with the company's objectives.

109

Be an Inspirational Leader

Leaders need vision, energy, authority, and a natural strategic ability. But those things don't necessarily help you inspire your employees to be their best and commit to you as a leader. Capture the hearts, minds, and spirits of your people with these qualities like:

- *Humanness*. Nobody wants to work with a perfect leader. Build collaboration and cooperation by revealing your weaknesses.
- *Intuition*. To be effective, you need to know what's going on without others spelling it out for you. Collect unspoken data from body language and looks given across rooms to help you intuit the underlying messages.
- *Tough empathy*. Care deeply about your employees,

but accept nothing less than their very best.

- *Uniqueness.* Demonstrate that you are a singular leader by showing your unique qualities to those around you.

110

Make the Right Hiring Decisions

Deciding who joins your organization or department can be a complex process. A bad decision has consequences not only for you as the hiring manager but for the new hire as well. Here are three ways to prevent a hiring disaster:

1. *Identify what the ideal candidate needs.* Too often managers set about hiring someone without outlining the competencies required for the job. Have a clear understanding of the skills that your hire needs to succeed.
2. *Understand motivation, not just experience.* Your candidate needs the right background and experience, but he or she also must have the right attitude. Ask interview questions that uncover the motivations behind past and future behavior.

3. *Help the new candidate onboard.* A "sink or swim" approach often results in drowning. Provide your new hire with support and a view into how things really work at your company. Give him or her early feedback on performance.

111

Improve Your Mission Statement

The problem with most mission statements, both business and personal, is that they are the same as the last guy's, full of empty and general words that apply to any organization or anyone. Boring ...

Many years ago, in a time and galaxy far, far away, I was looking for a job. I interviewed with three different GMs at three different companies, and they all said the same exact thing to me about their plans. It was like they all read the same book.

My point is, be creative, be innovative, and understand the direction and vision of your company so you can apply it intelligently. Thinking you understand is not enough. Get clarification and focus on action.

A mission statement is an abstract tool simply designed to keep you on track. It's not a strategic plan. An organization or individual on a mission is inspiring. Think about what it is you want and need to do: think differently, ask questions, understand whether the status quo is really okay. Change can be good or bad. There's a difference between managing and maintaining. Management requires a deliberate and constant motion. Make that your way. Missions and objectives can rally the troops, but only if they understand where they are going.

112

Don't Undermine the Process

Sometimes a colleague's agenda or actions may seem opposed to your own. It is then very easy to isolate and make that person out to be the bad guy—basically throwing a wrench into the spokes of productivity. Distorting or misrepresenting the motives of others is common when discomfort of another becomes evident or conflict comes. It's not particularly helpful in the long run. Internal competition may be healthy, but not to the point of disrupting productivity or solution focus. That's called *undermining the process*, and it actually works against you and your goals.

You need to exert influence in your realm, so instead of deciding that there's just something about certain colleagues you don't like, try to work your way into getting to know them better. Always work to influence, to stabilize, to correct, to think through, and to move things in the best interest of the organization.

113

Identify Talented People

Few are able to lead successfully without good talent supporting them. I have said this to you before: I'm only as good in my position as the people I surround myself by allow me to be. This goes for you too. Identifying your talented staff is not only good for the company, it's good for you as well. A few ways to keep those good people happy:

- *Know them.* Give your staff the opportunity to use their strengths. Do not hold them back. If you consider them a threat to you, well, then they *are* a threat to you. Your confidence should be the overriding factor.

- *Check in regularly.* Spend time talking with individuals to see how they're doing. It's so simple.

- *Recognize their strengths.* Know who is on your staff. How can they help you and help the company? What do they need to succeed? Know what assignments, perks, and recognition you can give.

114

Make Good Use of Your Time

What is time? It is the most perishable item you have. Once that second or minute has gone by, you will never get it back.

You have responsibilities, obligations, and things to do, like most. Meetings, more meetings … your boss calls, a customer or vendor calls … there can be little time to think and plan. This usually means that high-priority projects are delayed. The idea is to prioritize. The small stuff is easy. You should be able to distinguish what is really important from what can be dismissed or handled quickly so you can prioritize the "real." You've heard of time management? It's not an empty phrase. It distinguishes between the productive and the mundane. The high-priority issues or projects must be blocked off from the rest of your low-priority responsibilities or workload. How do you do that? Manage your time and create strategies, and then contingencies. Constantly work toward them. If you don't manage that time or use it efficiently, you'll lose it. It will be gone forever. Create value, understand decision-making, prioritize, and manage time.

115

Focus Yourself

How do you like what you do? This is an important question because it goes to your performance, interest, and attitude in your current or prospective position. It could be detrimental to your organization's goals or have a positive effect on them. Here are a few things to think about:

- *Are you doing what you want and like?* If you like what you are doing—the challenge, the fulfillment—think about that. If you don't like what you are doing, little moves forward, including ideas. Think about that.

- *What are your strengths and weaknesses?* Focus your energy on what you do well. We all complement each other's strengths and weaknesses. If you're in a position to delegate, then delegate—otherwise, you weaken your strengths by diluting them.

- *What are the strengths and weaknesses of others?* Think of this not as a way to ignore or dismiss, but as a way to enhance overall objectives—yours and the organization's.
- *What do you bring?* Consider your own value and what you contribute to the company.

116

Keep Your Goals in Perspective

Are you a boss, a leader? That means you have responsibilities to both your staff and the organization. Directing employees and helping them attain goals is part of your job. If your staff fails, it affects your goals, responsibilities, and obligations, and those of the organization. Lead yourself and your staff away from the possibility of failure by understanding the process of meeting the objective. Otherwise, it can and will cause problems for individuals, for you as the manager/leader, and for the organization. Keep your goals and that of your department in perspective and in the context of the overall objective of the organization.

Everything you do, every decision you make, impacts something. Have you ever heard of cause and effect? You need to be aware of your position as a leader and the impact it has on your staff, customers, and organization. You must develop your staff and connect it to the bigger picture.

117

Keep Your Vision in Sight

Does your company have a vision? Are you privy to it? It should and you should be—as a leader, it is your job and responsibility to create a vision for your organization or department. The trick is to get your staff to understand it and to get them on board. Try these steps:

1. *Communicate the vision.* Help your staff visualize the company's important goals.
2. *Move forward.* Once the vision is communicated effectively, ask for your staff's help. Be detailed in dialogue.
3. *Repeat the process.* Once you've completed the steps in communicating the vision to your staff, you must constantly relate to it in your decision-making. For example, if you are making a large

> or small decision that impacts a client, it should fit within the context of your vision, right? Are you concerned that your staff members will roll their eyes because you are repetitive? You shouldn't be. Constant reminders keep everyone on point and on track.

Now, here's the trick: even when you think you've communicated your vision perfectly and things are moving in the direction you assume you're supposed to be going in, you still need to stop and assess. It's akin to the way an aircraft's navigation system is constantly adjusting for wind and other factors, and then adjusting again. You need to do the same thing.

Your vision must be strategic.

118

Know How You Are Perceived

Have you ever thought about how others perceive you? Do you work a certain way and simply dismiss what other think or feel? We all have that thing about us that repels (or at least turns off) another. Obviously, we can't walk around the office trying to be liked or even change that way about ourselves that may be innate. However, there are some things you should try to do to affect your negative habits, such as:

- *Be aware of what you are doing and saying.* You can tell when someone is not exactly accepting you.
- *Know what you are thinking.* This you should be doing at all times so your mind does not wander into auto mode. If you know what you're thinking, you know what you are going to say or do.
- *Take a moment.* When you get that urge that you

> know may not be right—because you will feel it coming if you know what you're thinking—try and stop. Think. Breathe.

The idea here goes beyond perception and awareness. Working with others is a constant pull and push. Everyone has individual interests and motives. Your job is to work within this realm and be as productive as possible. There are constraints or advantages in this. The perception others have of you affects their behavior toward you. Human beings are social animals. Have you ever been on a bus or subway—a confined space with others you don't know—and notice someone looking at you … because you are looking right back? The reason is social; that's how we're wired. We need others. So you need to be aware of what perception others have of you, especially if it can affect your productivity in the workplace.

119

Appreciate Stress

Have you ever felt really stressed at work, or anywhere for that matter? Can you remember how you acted or reacted? Have you ever heard the expression, "A job without aggravation isn't really a job"? The fact is, you need stress once in a while to pique your senses, and this in turn may enhance your performance. It forces your brain to generate ideas and solutions, and improves your memory and intelligence. Simply stated, it can increase productivity. The idea here is not to look for stressful situations—this can have the opposite effect and stress you out, causing you to freeze or do something unreasonable. Don't look for stress, but understand it when you have it, and try to control it to your advantage.

120

Listen

Many plans, ideas, and thoughts fail because of communication—or more accurately, because the people involved are not paying attention. Listening is simply not there. You can imagine how frustrating that is for a leader, department head, or project manager. When someone is speaking with you, it is your responsibility to disseminate what is being conveyed, what is important, and what is not. Let's look at this in two ways:

- Your manager or superior, or colleague believes he or she has shared something important with you and that you have listened, and expects that your next step will be preparation. It's irrelevant whether your superior decided to move forward or not. His or her expectation is that you have listened to the communication and will move forward without waiting for more information. If you do not have this tuned in your brain, you need to change that.

- Your manager, superior, or colleague believes he or she has shared something important with you and that you have listened, and expects that your next step will be preparation. But, no ... you've actually blown them off and see no relevance, either because you don't care or you feel it's not important. However, if he or she is talking, then it is important to him or her. It is your responsibility to ask, and ask again, and then ask again until you understand and therefore are able to work through the idea, good or bad.

The issue here is that projects, ideas, and plans get stuck when you do not take things seriously or somehow believe you have the high ground by dismissing. This is a recipe for inaction, derailing, and simple blocking. It's a comfort zone that plays with others' time and efforts.

Do not assume another has heard you, either. If you have a doubt, your mind is telling you something. Move on it, communicate your point again, and make sure the other person got it, especially with those you know are defensive or resistant. Look for ways to improve your own communicating and listening skills.

121

Be Focused, but Not Too Focused

How do you perceive things around you? Have you ever thought about your tasks and the context in which you're performing them—in other words, how they may impact your colleagues' tasks or other issues you're not involved in directly? Well, being focused is good, but focused to the point of not considering the peripherals is not good. It's important to know what's going on around you and how your tasks and decisions are affecting others. A few ways to do that:

- *Look at the details.* But don't get stuck on them. To have the same idea rolling around in your head helps no one and reduces productivity.

- *Don't look for credit.* It forces you to focus on *you*, disturbing the good effect later. Don't worry, the people who matter see what you do.

- *Pull away.* Realize that you may be creating a redundant policy or procedure because you're looking at things too closely without appreciating or knowing what's going on in another department or in the organization as a whole.

122

Say "I Don't Know" (It Won't Kill You)

One of the worse things you can do is pretend that you know something when you don't. All it does is lead to more questions that you probably don't know the answer to, and it ultimately stalls a project, policy, procedure, or overall strategy. Not good.

You simply cannot know everything, and as an effective manager or leader you must surround yourself with people who do. That's what a leader does. Pretending that you know everything about everything creates a less-than-efficient department or organization and causes things to move forward with inaccuracies. And people know this. They know when you're pretending or bluffing your way through something, and it affects your leadership. Lose that, and good luck trying to win it back. Remember Clint Eastwood in *Magnum Force*? "A man's got to know his limitations." Well, same premise. It takes a real leader to say, "I don't know this."

123

Know What You Know

I am sure you have heard it many times: know what you're not good at, know your weaknesses. All kinds of factors interfere in assessing yourself, including ego. You may say to yourself, "Well, I may not be the best at this, but it's working, and I'm better at it than that guy." Well, no, you're not, and that's the trick, isn't it? Understanding this and allowing yourself to delegate or hand it off to someone who is more qualified than you at the task. It's not reducing yourself and admitting that your weakness applies to everything you do. It's simply accepting that this particular thing needs someone who either has a better understanding of it or is genetically in a better position to deal with it. Just accept that you need to hand it off.

Now, this does not mean you cannot or will not overcome a weakness of some sort. If you want to become fluent in something, study, read, or do what you can to improve. If it's not imperative, though, don't waste your time. That's what delegating's for.

Here's the important part: your position, job, organization, or what you are searching for may not be for you. There is nothing wrong with that. We all have our own equilibrium and cannot be good or interested in everything. You have strengths? Know what they are too. They will overcome your weaknesses.

124

Find Your Working Purpose

Do you enjoy going to work at all? If you dread Sunday nights, if you're groggy and unmotivated Monday mornings, if you're just getting the minimum done at your job, if you can't wait for the work day to be over, if you're not in the best of moods ... these are all signs of a lack of purpose.

You need to adjust your mindset, otherwise everything at the office becomes a chore. Once it's a chore, it becomes mechanical. Once it's mechanical, it becomes routine and the process of uncaring sets in. Your productivity drops, and so does that of the department or organization you work for.

Again, it's a mindset. You need to know your purpose regardless of the menial task you are performing. If you cannot pull out of the unproductive mindset, you must search for tasks that will shift that. What is your purpose? What is *the* purpose? These aren't religious questions ... they are questions you should simply be asking yourself.

125

Conduct Productive Meetings

There many different types of meetings: executive meetings, strategic meetings, micro-meetings, interdepartmental meetings ... the list goes on. They are sometimes considered one of the biggest wastes of time there is—not because they are unnecessary or pointless, but simply because attendees do nothing that specifically relates to them and connects them to an issue or to the clarity of a discussion. The point is missed.

Meetings have unfortunately become a nuisance and a chore in many cases. They are picked on because many times the focus is lost and the anticipated result is dismissed or not committed to. It takes a great deal of follow-up and task-planning to see the real value. Now, what *is* the real value? With anything, there is a process, and a follow-up to that process. How boring it is to say "the process," but that's exactly what it is: a process, the process of initiating and following up on issues. One decision in a direction affects another and inevitably forces another. The value comes from an effective strategy, implementing/executing, following up, and adjusting for unexpected circumstances.

The point is that meetings are necessary, and issues must move forward in the interest of finding a solution. Otherwise, status quo and maintenance become the norm, and overall competitiveness slows down in a market that does not stay still.

That said, the meeting-holders bear some responsibility in conducting productive agendas that are intended to move the organization or department forward. (The constant in any business is that if you are not moving forward, you are dying.) Moving forward is impossible if the agendas are recurring because of lack of movement by attendees.

Your strategic planning is important within the context of your objectives based on the meeting's agenda. Do not allow yourself to idle.

126

Get Moving

"I'm going to get that done right away." "I'll get on that tomorrow." "I'll get moving on this soon." The interesting thing about these statements is that most of us believe ourselves—so much so that we can even project, picture, or imagine the task being completed or the issue resolved. Why? Because it all seems so easy when you talk about it; even if you've created a strategy, it comes across as achievable. But of course it is, because your mind has already worked through the process. So the next steps you take is ... none at all, or a deliberate push to do what you've set out to do.

Excuses are easy to create because they need no proof, they are easily manipulated, and most of all, they are the perfect way to either blame someone else for inaction or convince yourself that an issue is dismissible.

Actually *doing* something entails initiative, commitment, thought, momentum, ambition, and drive. Doing encourages the mind to think, learn, innovate, create, and motivate. All of these words may sound like self-help tools, but they are actually built into you already; all you need to do is access them, apply them, and *do*. There's a time for talking, and there's a time for doing.

The world around you is fraught with naysayers, barriers, and derailers. Your job is to push through it and get things done. Will it happen overnight? Never. Stay tenacious to your objectives, and you will accomplish them. We're talking about in the office, in business; how you apply this to your personal life is up to you. The idea here is to move on things instead of just having an idea about things. Talking and thinking but not changing anything may feel good, but it accomplishes absolutely nothing.

Managing a to-do list is completely different from having a wish list. Write things down in an organized form, or get it into your Outlook with benchmarks. Keep the processes flowing. Understand that there is a reason and a purpose. At some point, after the wheel was invented, someone said, "Wait a minute, what if we put a chassis on this thing?" Okay, maybe not the best analogy, but you get the point. One thing leads to another. Talking leads to more talking.

127

Speak Up

Whether you're in an executive-committee meeting or a one-on-one, speak up! Why? Because if you do not speak up, you will be led. Now, let's bring this into context. This is not to suggest that you challenge issues based on your confidence in something, just that you should speak up when you have an idea. No one has a monopoly on ideas. It's important that they flow fluidly and that environments are created to encourage them.

Your thoughts and opinions will never be heard, and your ability to influence direction will be mooted, simply because of your lack of speaking up. Not every idea is a good idea; not every idea will work in the context of a specific issue. However, one idea generates another and then another.

Understand that how you present and convey your idea is as important as the idea itself; the idea will be considered on the basis of its delivery. Once an idea is conveyed, allow for feedback. Don't try to hoard or dominate the issue. Pulling back a little will allow others to build on your idea and share the risk—and the success.

Sell your point, because no one can do it like you can.

128

Choose to Delegate

When to delegate and how is the question. You need to balance what your responsibilities are and what you're being asked to do. In business, speed is of the essence. If you're stuck because you have not delegated properly or efficiently, then your work is being done inefficiently. (Example: Why do you think executives hire administrative assistants? Because they've arrived? No. It's because the delegation of specific tasks allows executives to be more efficient in their work, so they are not bogged down.) You may get your tasks done, but not in a timely manner. Believe me, it's noticed.

So how do you do it? As you're moving forward on a task or project, inevitably it's going to put you in contact with someone else. Whether you delegate to that someone else or not will determine how effective you really are. Delegate correctly, and that piece of information or part of the overall project will move smoothly. Do it wrong, and you'll simply look like you're pawning off work. Follow these steps for successful delegation.

1. *Before:* Understand and create a strategy for what you need to accomplish. Who's involved? This does not mean create a strategic planning memo, it simply means work the steps through your head.
2. *During:* How is the work moving along? What tasks are others more qualified (or in a better position) to complete for you? Monitor the progress by working through the issues with the persons you've delegated to.
3. *After:* Whatever is being delegated needs to be for a purpose ... and that purpose is efficiency and productivity. The task or project should be completed in a timely way, or why delegate at all?

This may sound simple in theory, but I assure you that delegating is not something everyone feels comfortable with. Getting comfortable with it is important in your ability to get things done.

129

Turn Your Ideas into Reality

You have an idea; you may think it's a great idea, or you may think it through a bit and realize that it's a stupid idea. What should be realized is that there are reasons why many ideas fail and reasons why many succeed.

It's not easy to convince others that your idea is the right one. Your think-through and confidence play an important role. If you give up easily and your idea fails, you may have set up failure for you next idea, because your approach is not thorough or convincing. Not all ideas require an empirical backing. Sometimes just getting others to imagine your idea and believe in its benefits is enough. How do you do this?

- Present your ideas calmly and confidently.
- Don't give up on an idea too easily—rethink, and then try it again if you're still convinced.

- Know when enough is enough. Understand futility.
- Know the persons you are conveying your idea to. Understanding what they are about will help you mold your idea to their thinking.
- Think through the others' arguments and naysaying. Your idea should be thought through in a larger context.
- Don't be aggressive and pushy, but be influential.
- Never run out of ideas.

130

Manage Properly and Securely

So you have your staff, and you have your boss or board that you are accountable to. Your staff, under your delegation or directive, is working on projects and policies that, in your mind, are all designed to increase the performance of your department or company. How do you manage your staff? There are two types of managers:

1. The micromanaging type, who thinks he or she must stay on top of the staff to ensure performance that will reflect on the manager ultimately.
2. The open type, who communicates with staff and makes sure there is a clear understanding of the direction and desired goal or outcome.

The first manager is in for a hard time. Micromanaging is fraught with negative repercussions, from a disgruntled staff to little room for flexibility if something goes wrong (and it will). The people you've chosen to surround yourself with are the people who will make or break your goals. If you micromanage them, the question to ask yourself is, "Am I stifling their creativity and growth?" Allow me to answer that: yes, you are. Why did you hire or promote them in the first place?

Manage properly and securely. Communicate what needs to get done, and then leave them alone to do it. This does not mean walk away and whatever comes of it comes of it. That would be a disaster also. Then the question would be, "Why do they need you?"

Monitor your staff, give guidance, give support, give input, and give flexibility. Ask the right questions that help place the direction. That's how you manage your staff.

131

Keep Your Ego in Check

This is something simple, but we all can forget at times, especially in the heat of the moment. Many times our ego is misplaced—meaning that although we've worked hard to get where we are, it does not mean we have a right to arrogance. Sometimes you are the beneficiary of circumstance or the victim of circumstances. Whatever the issue, whatever the case, when dealing with your colleagues and subordinates, remember who you are. Remember that cooperation and the simplicity of helping others are paramount to success.

I believe I've mentioned this before: the United States (the American culture) was founded on individual means. From when we were children, we've been taught this. It's a good thing—it promotes self-reliance and ambitious behavior. But this should not get in the way of what is right. What is right? Keeping your ego in check and being ethical toward others. It promotes a much more productive environment. The office is a place in which you spend a lot of time. Enough said.

132

Listen to Your Doubt

Can you remember when you were in school, and a question on a test came up that you were unsure about? Later, your marked test would come back, and sure enough, the question you were unsure about was answered wrong. Now, why did this happen? The simplest answer is that you didn't study. But assuming you are responsible and you did study, the reason you got it wrong was that you overanalyzed and did not question your doubt. Your doubt is your inner instinct telling you to question something and change it if necessary.

Important decisions are not easy, especially when they involve or impact other people. Think about these things when making your decisions:

- *Don't overanalyze.* Analyze, yes, but when you overanalyze, all you are doing is questioning yourself further. That creates more doubt, and you will end up more confused than helpful.

- *Know yourself.* Your prejudgments and life experiences play a big role in your decisions. Understand yourself and your motives.
- *Doubt.* When you have a doubt, stop and think. Your instincts, your gut, are telling you something.

133

Be Aware of Your Surroundings

Finding yourself in a hard place because you played the political game wrong? It happens quite often. You think you're in the know, but you aren't, and the result is that you've impaired yourself for the next round. Remember that it is much easier to destroy than to create or repair. Your efforts need to be honed in a number of areas.

This may sound cynical, and your first reaction may even be, "I don't play politics. I go to work and do my job." Well, perhaps—but if you don't think politics plays a role in your advancement or lack thereof, it's important that you look up the word *naive*.

Human beings are social and political animals. Being aware of your surroundings is crucial to how you are perceived by others and how you interact with others—who, by the way, all have their own motives. Because we are social, our eyes are constantly scanning others, pulling in information both subtly and overtly. Don't get me wrong, this does not mean everyone is scheming, but it does mean that at some level, they've judged something and will react at that moment or later, positioning themselves in a place that best meets their interests.

It's risky business, because you either move forward or stay still.

134

Realize Advisors Are Only Giving Advice

They're all good people, well-educated, well-intentioned, but lawyers, accountants, and consultants are the epitome of caution, and make suggestions without knowing all the facts or intricacies of a business—which is unique in both culture and operations. Admire their efforts and knowledge, but accept their advice as just that: advice. They are not always correct, and it is imperative to put your understanding of your circumstances and needs first. Remember, caution is in their nature.

135

Keep Your Mind Moving

Have you ever had an idea? Of course you have … you always do. Our minds are constantly asking. The problem is convincing others. No one likes being rejected, but approaching it right can soften the blow if your idea is rejected, and places you in a position where others will listen to another idea later. Follow these tips:

- *Devise a strategy.* Your idea needs to have a strategy behind its necessity. Change is not something people like, even if they say they do. It's arduous for most because it involves effort and thinking. Your idea needs to be convincing in a way that makes it seem not only simple but quite necessary.

- *Don't be pushy.* No one likes to be made to feel like an idiot. Don't tell others of an idea you have and make it look like you're the smartest person in the room for thinking of it. Believe me, you'll need their help to get it done.

- *Be realistic.* The worse thing to do is to think your idea will change the world, convincing yourself that nothing at all is wrong with it. Implementation requires steps. Make sure you go into things humbly and patiently.

The most important thing, however, is not to stop thinking. Your mind should be moving always, because even the littlest change in your work habits generates more ideas.

136

Be Confident

Confidence is attractive to others, because we all have moments of self-doubt. Believe it or not, even people in very high posts or positions question themselves, asking, "How did I get here?" It's good in a way, because it shows some humility. However, confidence is more than likely the reason they are where they are, even if they doubt themselves sometimes. There are several ways to help yourself build and secure confidence, including:

- *Self-analysis*. What are you good at? Do you know, or do you just bluff your way through things hoping for the best? That's good enough. Being wrong enough times can kill anyone's confidence. Analyze yourself, and know what you know how to do well.

- *Process*. Have you ever heard the expression, "It's

the process"? Well, it is. How about, "Practice makes perfect"? Well, it does—but only if you have the equilibrium for it. (Honestly, if you're not good at it, then you're not good at it.) Practicing and studying is where experience and knowledge come in. That's what builds confidence.

- *Search.* Look around and think about what you like to do. As mentioned above, if you don't have the equilibrium for it, you will have a hard time succeeding at it, and that will suppress your confidence. I know your parents used to tell you, "You can do whatever you set out to do." They were not telling you the truth. You need to know what you are good at, work at it, discipline yourself, and your confidence will kick in. It's a good feeling, being confident. (With a little humility.)

137

Save Us from Disorganized Restructuring

Results that are less than obvious are good for no one. Not for customers, not for you, not for your managers or line staff, not for morale, not for anything. When managers overhaul their teams, the question becomes, to what end or result? Restructuring or reorganization means nothing if it's effort only. A deliberate movement forward with a cohesive and shared objective is what brings tangible results. The lack of action—and especially, the lack of a strategy or plan—simply gives the appearance of things getting done, without actually doing anything. Worse, complicated, dysfunctional, and disorganized patterns take hold, wasting human resources, creativity, and productivity. Here are a few ways to stay focused:

- *Take a step back and analyze what's happening around you.* Are you utilizing your managers properly? Is your structure set up properly? What's your plan? Is it on paper somewhere for your own reference? Do you and your managers really know what the objectives are, and are you all in sync?

- *Do not adjust for personalities.* Instead, help them assimilate into the strategy. People are what make things happen, but they can be the problem too. Hold your managers and staff accountable—they are not children, and what is expected from them is grown-up behavior and accountability to the actions and responsibilities of their positions.

- *Be flexible.* Rigidity comes from two-dimensional thinking. You must have a strategy, but you must allow it to evolve.

- *Take your responsibilities seriously.* Yes, your job should be something you enjoy ... but only you can make it enjoyable. There is something called Serious Fun. Concentrate on where the organization is going, and enjoy making it happen.

138

Set a Tone with Your Behavior

I've said it before: if you cannot change the person, change the environment to influence the behavioral change you seek. Not easy to do, but doable. Do you know how and what a culture is or how it's formed? It's simply a process over time that has created a collective behavioral pattern. You can create as many policies as you want demanding certain behavior, but it simply will not change the culture.

Behavior is contagious. You must set your own tone and create the successes that your staff will see and respect. Define your responsibilities and coordinate those responsibilities with other executive-committee members and managers. Your vision, based on the company's vision, must be conveyed to your subordinates. Think about the overall culture of your organization, think about your department's culture, envision what you want, and then manifest it. Again, not easy, but doable with focus.

Human Resources is a corporate and managerial tool. Organizational processes funnel through HR, which helps create necessary guidance for you and your staff alike. Use this tool to help make the cultural changes you envision.

139

Manage Performance

When managing overall performance, there are a few things that you should consider:

- *Assess the progress of your objectives constantly.* But not to the point of over-managing.
- *Know what your competitors are doing.* Simply being happy with your results does nothing to help you stay on your game. Remember, you are not the center of it all. Look outward. What are the customers saying?
- *Move forward.* Although the past is important for learning, it's not important for copying. The past is past. Focus on the future by strengthening your competitive advantages, by being creative, by managing performance.

- *Take care of your customers, and your customers will take care of you.* This does not mean just smile and be nice and they'll return. It means understanding their need and rolling with it; staying on top of what they are saying, demanding, and asking; and constantly assessing and measuring the results of your actions. Looking at and understanding the numbers and making smart decisions based on them is important, but it's not the only measurement. You have to be cognizant of what's happening around you—within your company or department and with your customers. Quantify and qualify.

140

Criticize Carefully

Even the most skilled managers have difficulty giving criticism. But as a manager or leader, you must. It's not easy telling people that they talk too much, or that they need to dress more professionally, or that they need to refine their speech or writing skills. It should be helpful to them, but as human beings we all have an ego and feelings. Inevitably, the subordinate you've spoken to will be insulted. Do not fret. You are being helpful, and your conveyance of this information is in the interest of the company and ultimately their interest. Keep these points in mind:

- The way you say things is important. Give criticism privately and with understanding.
- Don't bury what you are trying to say. Be as straightforward as you can.
- Be consistent with criticism and positive feedback.

141

Focus on the Task at Hand

You've heard of time management, I'm sure. Task management is just as critical to your efficiency. You've complained about not having enough time ... but that means you are probably hurrying through tasks, creating loose ends. Loose ends are details, and details are too important to be loose.

What you need to do is focus on the task at hand and have a strategy to complete it. Try creating a to-do list. You need to be able to think your way through a task to its end. Otherwise, the details become disorganized, and then good luck trying to complete the task accurately. Go through this process:

1. *Think about the task.* Go through it with your goal or objective in mind.
2. *Write it down on your to-do list.* Check off as you reach benchmarks or complete parts of it.

Simple, right? Simplicity works. The thoroughness and detailed way you complete a task says a lot.

142

Don't Get Bogged Down

The definition of *bogged down* is "to be hindered or slowed." The question is, do you know if you're bogged down? In the most obvious ways, you do. For example, if your car is stuck in the mud, you know you're bogged down. There's no forward progress.

Now let's apply that same term to your personal life. You have an idea about something you would like to accomplish. But you get home from work, begin taking care of dinner, maybe go shopping, walk the dog, take care of a child, maybe do some cleaning .... This is pretty much what you'd call a routine. However, if you're ambitious, or if you have important things to accomplish and find that they're not happening, then your routine is bogging you down. You will wake up one day and be in the same spot.

Now let's apply the same term to your professional life. You have responsibilities to your supervisor and your staff. Think for a moment. Are you moving forward? Are you applying yourself and utilizing the power and authority you have to move forward? Are you managing your human resources properly? Thinking you are does not mean it's true. Excuses are not progress. Are you managing your time and tasks? Are you serious about it?

One of the great things about the human mind is our imagination. It drives us forward or it fools us into falling behind. If you cannot benchmark, you are not moving forward. If you come into work and the problem you had yesterday and the day before still exists, you are not moving forward. You are allowing yourself to be bogged down; you are moving through a created process that will not be broken away from because your thinking has not changed.

Break out of it, or come in tomorrow only to realize it's Groundhog Day, again.

143

Try Internal Networking

You've heard the word *networking* used to describe computers communicating with each other, or the networking of friends and colleagues in different companies or industries for social and professional reasons. But what about internal networking? It's imperative to building your experience and to the success of your department and the organization. Some ways to do it:

- *Understand the people you are working with.* If your motives are sincere, they will pick up on that.

- *Network smartly.* It's not the quantity of people you network with, it's the quality.

- *Identify new blood for new ideas.* There's nothing worse than networking with someone who has little motivation, a disinterest in cultivating relationships, or a habit of making excuses. People get set in their ways when they are in a position for too long, and many times that will derail change or ideas. This is not good for your morale. It's best to find others who share your sense of direction and can help you follow it.

144

Ask Yourself, "What Am I Good At?"

As a manager and leader, your areas of focus have changed since you were on the way up. Your focus now should always be on the organization's needs, not your own.

There are certain things you cannot do. Each of us has strengths and weaknesses, each of us has our equilibrium. You are not good at everything, and the biggest mistake is to think you are. Managers and leaders look at the bigger picture and do what they are good at. The rest is delegated, which is why you have support staff. If your employees are incapable of performing, they need to be held accountable. Accountability counts.

The key here is to know yourself and focus on what you know how to do.

145

Have a Plan

Do you simply go from day to day hoping, thinking, rolling along? You should know where you are going. What's that saying, again? "The road to Somewhere led to a town called Nowhere." In other words, if you don't have a vision, plan, or strategy for the future, you will simply end up somewhere that is either someone else's direction or the same place you are today. Understand this: if you do not discipline yourself, someone will do it for you. It's simple psychology and can be applied both personally and professionally. You should have your to-do list with your objectives and benchmarks. This helps you stay focused and on point for the most part. But what about what's in your head? You need an overall master plan or strategy that's constantly evolving—pulling you forward, so to speak.

When your mind is moving, it generates ideas, allowing you to focus on something new, something beneficial, and something rewarding. When applying this to your professional life, your job, what do you envision? Or do you have a low sense of urgency, or maybe a *manana* syndrome?

Don't be like most people who simply go through work or life just to get through the day. Have a plan, a strategy for yourself that coordinates your vision and efforts with that of your organization. Apply this personally, too, and you will see progress in both areas of your life.

Remember that even the best plans go astray, but when you are thinking and adjusting, staying focused on the objective, your plan will naturally adapt.

146

Follow Through

What are the factors that prevent you from deciding? Think about them for a moment. What is the impact of you not deciding? Think about that too. Allow me to give you two outcomes:

1. Paralysis
2. Status quo

A CEO of a large American company was recently asked by his wife, "How was your meeting today?"

His answer was, "Well, we all talked a lot, but nothing was decided or accomplished."

You must make decisions and then follow through with them. You must engage in discussions with your managers and line staff to ensure clarity. Then you must follow-up again. Speak directly with people, in a decisive manner.

147

Be Aware of Your Conditioning

Your mind and your actions are conditioned by the past—not the present and not the future. The past reflects your present decisions and future planning. Think about this clearly for a moment. Everything you do today comes from your mind and your actions, reflecting something that's happened before and interpreting it into what you do now. It's almost automatic. The only way to break this pattern somewhat (because it cannot be completely dismissed) is to be aware of yourself and what's happening around you. I've said it before: know what you are thinking.

How do we translate this into our business goals? Being conditioned means being in conflict with problems that arise. Your past experiences may cause caution and fear. Being uncertain and attempting to predict restricts creative thinking, planning, and strategizing. Attachment to the ways you know limits your ability to appreciate what's truly possible. As social beings, we communicate and cooperate to instill a sense of progress and shared goals, hence results. The opposite of this is holding on and looking to be secure, as we all want to be. The process is basic to everything we consider and every decision we make. We search for a reference that is not always helpful. We settle, accept, and endure, at the cost of inaction.

When we are aware of the larger picture, so to speak, a barrier can be broken down where immediate solutions that remove us from the impending discomfort of a problem or issue can be dealt with in a less confrontational or uncooperative way. How do we do this more specifically? Well, it's not easy. But if you understand the problem and take the time to see it objectively, with a focus on the intricacies of the issue, then a solution can be presented much more easily, with less resistance. Why? Because you are aware and understand.

Try to look at your obligations and responsibilities in this way so you can move forward unimpeded by grudges and nonsense. Your competitors are not without their own problems. You should be taking advantage of that by organizing and implementing for your future success.

148

Make the Most of Time, Money, and Resources

How do you make your decisions when it comes to the company's time, money, and resources? Ultimately, the results will tell you how you're doing. For example, when it comes to time, are you using some type of time-management technique? When it comes to purchasing, are you looking at the costs and necessities of the purchase? Are you making scheduling decisions—or any decisions, for that matter—based on efficiency? Are you allocating human or material resources using the proper assumptions? Have you at least figured out an ROI? Your title demands that you look at these things in the most important way; you must force yourself not to be satisfied with simple or lateral results.

Think your decisions through so that the company's time, the company's money, and the company's resources are not being wasted. The company counts on you, as you count on the company.

149

Humble Yourself

Do you know everything? I doubt it ... and if you think you do, or if you think you're the smartest one in the room, then you need to humble yourself ASAP.

As a leader, you may naturally have strong feelings of confidence. The trick is to not be arrogant about it, and to understand your place. Authority does not need to be advertised to be effective, and understanding that you do not have a monopoly on ideas goes a long way.

Most of us dislike authority. Not in a hostile way, but in a hindering way. I don't think there's anyone who likes to be told what to do in a command-and-control manner. You do not want your staff to be afraid of you. You want them to respect your vision, respect your departmental and organizations goals, respect *you*.

Ask your subordinates for their opinion on issues (more so your managers, who are in the thick of it) and allow productive disagreement with your decisions, policies, or process. Being challenged on an issue is not a bad thing if it's done in a productive and constructive way. Your job is to instill that belief in your managers and subordinates.

The next question is: Do you feel threatened when you are questioned? If so, not good. It shows insecurity.

150

Form Relationships with the Right People

Do you know the saying, "It's whom you know, not what you know?" Well, guess what? It's true. Now, don't take this out of context to mean that you can be a non-thinker or a non-doer and you will still make it. What it means is that your relationships with the right people are critical to your growth. You can be an ace at what you do, but not getting along with the right people or getting involved in silly interoffice gossip will only delay, derail, or slow your efforts because the people you should be aligning yourself with will be unimpressed, looking past your stellar work and only at your less-than-focused behavior. Maybe that's not fair, but that's the way it is. Politics and relationships make the world go round. Here are a few tips:

- *Know what your responsibilities are and focus on them.* Who around you can help or support you in your responsibilities and efforts? That's where your relationships should be formed ... but avoid forming an obvious clique.

- *Realize that everyone has an agenda.* That does not mean it is a malicious agenda; someone may be vying for influence, someone may be just trying to make it through the day to get home to family, someone may be ambitious and attempting to impress. The point is, find the ones who share your passion for success or direction. Stay clear of the ones who are obviously disruptive, with no clear ambition or direction.

- *Seek people who help you find balance.* Working, thinking about work, and dreaming about work is not balance. People who share things like books and conversation with you stimulate you mentally, encourage you professionally, and care about you—the ones you're able to speak to openly and without tension—are the ones who help you achieve balance.

If you think about this, it's actually a networking strategy. It's a good thing that will help you succeed.

151

Get Promoted

Promotion is not for everyone. We all have our priorities in life, and sometimes additional responsibilities and better compensation are not sought after. However, if you are ambitious and seek growth, there are certain things you need to be aware of.

An office environment is filled with different personalities, and navigating your way through these personalities is not always easy. Also, you can rest assured that the powers that be are watching, even if it does not seem so. There are no written rules for who is going to be promoted and who is not. On the contrary, although some organizations may have an internal matrix system in place to guide in such matters, the process is vastly more dependent on how you are performing—or perceived to be performing—within a larger context. What are the decision-makers seeing?

- *Your conduct:* How you conduct yourself in the workplace is integral to how you are perceived and how you get along with peers, colleagues, and bosses.

- *Your performance:* Do you blame others when something does not go your way? That's not what a leader does. Your performance is yours: *you* are accountable and responsible. Can you imagine that a position you want in the organization opens up, and when you're interviewing for it you say, "Well, I could have done this or that, but he or she blocked me, or he or she wasn't doing their job"? It does not work.

- *Your integrity:* You need integrity. Your organization is desperate for leaders with integrity. Focus on organizational needs.

- *Your ambition:* Simply, do you have it? It's a virtue, and if channeled properly—watch out.

Again, being promoted is not for everyone, and that's okay. But if it's what you seek, be aware of your behavior, be aware of your performance, be aware of your responsibilities.

152

Just Ask

Questions are so important, but we just do not take advantage of the opportunities and benefits questions bring to our performance during a normal day's work. Some people are shy about asking questions, some have large egos and won't allow themselves to ask questions, some are afraid to ask questions for whatever reason, and some just feel that they shouldn't ask. Avoiding questions is the worst thing you can do. People have an innate desire to help others. It's just a natural thing. Ask.

153

Play the Game

Politics is something we watch on television and usually feel disgust about. But did you know that politics is everywhere, including where you work? *Especially* where you work.

Do you think avoiding office politics is the right thing to do? It's not. You need to manage, navigate, and play the game, or you'll find yourself in an inadequate position. Worse yet, you'll get stepped on. The game is not to be played in a mean-spirited or nasty way, but as a way to get things done.

When you get home at night, your dinner-table conversation should not be, "Well, I had a wonderful day at the office, speaking with no one, and I got the minimum done." It should be, "Well, it was a great day! I was very effective in getting certain things done today—it wasn't easy, but I moved things forward."

Politics is just the way it is, a part of being human. There's no other way. It's not a bad thing, and if the game is played correctly and intelligently, you come out ahead and fulfilled. There's a difference between playing the game to agitate people or to be more efficient at what you do. Pick the latter.

154

Question Yourself

As you manage, your mind should be in constant fluidity. As you're working on a project or running a department, the questions you ask yourself should be in the context of creativity, innovation, improvement, and simplicity. It's a skill, because when you're asking yourself the right questions and extending those questions to those around you, exciting answers and positive results will result. An accomplishment presented to the benefit of your clients is good business, and good for you. Ask:

- How can I balance, manipulate, convert, or change the direction so it inspires those around me and myself?
- How can I create a momentum that continues to influence the process without negative pushback?

- How can I build a structure that improves productivity, processes, and experiences?

People count on you to lead, to manage. Do it.

155

Deal Directly with Poor Behavior

One of the most frustrating things to witness is poor behavior from subordinates, colleagues, or unions. This can come in many forms: tirades, irrational statements, refusal to follow policies and procedures, rudeness, sabotage, deliberate derailing, resistance to change. Even just writing the words is frustrating. However, there is a way you can deal with this, through self-discipline and training. Management needs to be on the same page with this so a predictable response is the norm. Deal with problem behavior this way:

- *Nip it in the bud.* Have you heard of a sixth sense we all supposedly have? The next time you have a doubt or something seems off, you are probably right. Control your thoughts, know what you are thinking, and then address the matter as rationally as you can. Remember that your concerns are more about anticipation than the actual matter at hand. Deal with the subordinate, colleague, or union representative in a manner of rational containment.

- *Be rational.* But don't demand that the other person be rational. Understand the psychology of what is happening. That person has an interest, a point of view, an opinion, an insecurity they are attempting to vent or release. Listen, regardless of inaccuracies, and in a rational, quiet tone respond and attempt to move your position forward.

- *Think.* There must be a reason for the person to be behaving a certain way. What is it? It's your job to figure it out and attempt to correct it. Here is a hint: it is most certainly based on a previous experience. Deal with the issues in a rational tone, respond, and attempt to move your position forward.

I know—easier said than done. But discipline and training will minimize hostility, confrontation, and disruptive behavior.

156

Focus on What's Happening Today

Look at your P&L and balance sheet and try to explain to a board or executive committee what it all means—how if this number did this and that number did that the big number on the bottom would be bigger. Bad idea. There is just no way you can run a business or department by analyzing the financials to death and making assumptions based on that. Now, that's not to say that the financials are not important. They are absolutely imperative as a lagging indicator of the company or department's inefficiencies and low productivity. However, they cannot tell you what's underneath the dysfunction or the intangibles of why you're running inefficiently. That's something you must know as a manager or leader.

You must be aware and concerned about what is happening today:

- What are your customers telling you?

- What behavioral changes do you see coming?
- What kind of technology can you use to stay on top of trends?
- What policies and procedures do you have in place that may be hindering growth or customer satisfaction?

These are only some of the questions you should be asking yourself every day. Your financials can only have you guessing afterward—too late. Focus on what's happening today and understand the impact of your direction. Then, the financials will tell you that you're doing something right. But ultimately it's you and your decisions doing that.

157

Create a Cooperative Process

You're doing everything right. You come to work, get your responsibilities done just the way they're supposed to be. You're the smart one in the office, and everyone else is having issues because, well, they are just not as smart as you, right?

Nice try, but you're wrong. It's like leaving your wingman because you think you can get it done on your own. Meanwhile, you've disadvantaged others on your team. Get where I'm going here?

It's okay to move aggressively on things and make them happen—you want a promotion or more pay or fulfillment or whatever floats your boat. However, by thinking you're the smartest person in the room and flying solo, you actually undermine the whole process and contradict what your responsibilities are in the first place. When issues come back to you, it's not because the other person is not as smart as you, it's because you've created a sphere for yourself. Disengage your solo mentality and create a cooperative process. Watch how much gets done.

158

Know What Things Cost

There is nothing more frustrating than getting ripped off, or just thinking that you got ripped off. How would you know? You should have an understanding of what things cost and what benefit they bring. It sounds simple enough, but few do a cost-benefit analysis even in its simplest form. Here are some questions to ask:

- *Why am I investing in this?* It can't just be a toy. Whatever it is, look at its cost closely and determine whether it will pay for itself either in efficiency or direct savings.

- *Will I need to reinvest?* If you are purchasing something at a certain cost now, will you need to maintain, upgrade, or replace it at a future date? What's that cost? Should you spend more to alleviate that issue, and if so, did you reevaluate the cost benefit?

- *Am I saving anything at all?* It's a simple question, and one you should know the answer to.

- *When will I see the results of the purchase?* There should be a measureable time after which you anticipate a return. This is where your financials are important.

- *What are the intangibles?* Some things can be measured easily. Others cannot, and you will need to have a strong argument for yourself and your boss as to why there is a benefit to your decision. That part is not easy. Know what you're talking about. Know your math.

159

Create a Strategy Before, Not After

A strategy is something you create before you begin a project or implement a new policy or procedure. People make mistakes, implementation is sloppy, you forgot something … all of this is well and dandy, as we all know, because we're all human. But mistakes and waste can be minimized with a series of steps that involve a little more thinking and help from your staff:

1. Write down on a piece of paper a point-by-point task list.
2. Next to each point, write down the navigation aspects.
3. Meet with your staff and get their ideas.
4. Anticipate issues. Something will not go the way you had laid it out.

5. Prepare to adjust as you are moving forward.

Advance planning is critical, because reacting to something that's already happened creates doubts, can be expensive, wastes time, and frankly makes you look unprepared.

Having a strategy and focusing on it allows you to control the outcome. Bouncing around in mid-task trying to fix things or get them back on track makes you look like you don't know what you're doing. You know what to do ...

160

Change Your Behavior

Why can't Jim get things done like Ralph? Why can't Sally do things differently? It's because everyone has strengths and weaknesses. If you want to change something, start with yourself. You don't need a New Year's resolution to change your behavior or your way of thinking. (And by the way, that way of thinking may be holding you back from a promotion, higher compensation, or both.) Think about it honestly:

- Are you afraid of being more aggressive? If so, why?
- Do you want everyone to like you?
- Do you lack the confidence to be more aggressive?
- Are you moving too fast?
- Are you too critical of others?

- Are you impatient with others? Why?
- Do you think you're the smartest one in the room?
- Do you think that if you slow down, others may think you're not doing your job?

These are questions that you can either answer, dismiss, or expand on, but the point is, you need to look at things within the perspective and context that others are involved with things you are doing, and they do things differently than you do. Have you ever heard that expression, "A horse has its own mind—if it wants to go that way, it's going to go that way"? Well, human beings are worse. The difference is that you're a human being, so you can deal with other human beings in a more meaningful and productive way. That means you don't have to try to change everything that you disagree with or have an issue with.

You need to be smart and adjust your behavior where and when necessary. Understanding yourself and the areas you know deep down you can change is not that difficult to do. We are creatures of habit and routine. If you practice the changes you want to make in yourself, day after day, week after week, soon they will become natural to you. You must have a strategy for yourself; you must know what you are thinking and control what you are thinking. Got it?

161

Realize It's Not All About You

So you're trying to get things done, moving them along, because ultimately it's a reflection on you when things are not going the way they are supposed to. And it's true, you have these people on your team or in your department who just don't get it. When you are angry, it's fairly easy to start attacking; you vent, and the conversation becomes all about your needs and why *you* need to get these things done.

Although it may not seem like the easiest way, you should pull that person into your office and focus on his or her needs, not yours. If your employees are supposed to feel that they have a say, that you are interested in their success, that you want them to have the right tools, that they have your support, that they understand your direction or vision, this is what will turn them around—not talking to them about how they are screwing things up for you.

162

Be the Leader Your Employees Deserve

First and foremost, the question is, "What is the purpose of managers and management?" The answer is, to create policies and procedures that are predictable, benefiting both employee understanding and productivity. In other words, your staff needs to know that they have a leader, someone who does not create confusion because of insecurities or indecisiveness. Your responsibility as a manager or team leader is intertwined with the performance of your subordinates. In a sense, you are responsible for their success. And believe me, if they understand this because they see and sense it, the staff's productivity level will increase. Your team must have a sense of trust, focus, appreciation, purpose, strategy, confidence, and reassurance that you believe in them by supporting their position. This goes back to "it's not all about you."

Keep them interested while you are conducting the responsibilities of a leader, which also includes working on the periphery of the implemented policies and procedures.

163

Remember Slow and Steady Wins the Race

Being anxious and or impatient at times is natural. But in business, things need to move at a pace that allows all areas of the business to catch up or be prepared. In other words, whether you're involved in a turnaround, setting up a new business, or implementing a new policy or procedure, you need to work in a steady and deliberate manner. Any efforts to force a particular element forward will backfire. That's the way businesses work. The slow and steady pace at which one needs to move assures that the intricacies and accuracies of what you are attempting to accomplish will be done properly. Hurry it, rush it, and it will come back.

164

Keep Looking for Something to Do

If you stop looking for something to do, you find yourself later with nothing to do. Many people are content to maintain the status quo and watch the world go by. The problem with that is, the world *will* go by. The sun will rise in the morning, and you will have a new name: Yesterday.

Look for things to do. Improve, compete, create, initiate, start, contemplate your next move. If you don't move forward, you're falling back.

165

Don't Hesitate

Put yourself in an indecisive position for a moment. Think about a time when you were not decisive, like hesitating while crossing a street or making a financial decision and then changing your mind, having remorse. When you hesitate, you allow something else to happen. It's really a form of freezing while everything around you keeps going. It can be dangerous, or just a few seconds of wasted time. I'm not suggesting that it's unnatural to hesitate; we all have instincts that help us avoid danger. But by hesitating and not moving decisively on something, you create an opportunity that doesn't include you.

Changing your mind after you've made a decision can also be detrimental. Once you have made a decision, you have created an inertia and momentum. Can you know the outcome? Not completely, but you have an idea of it because you are driving it. When you change midstream, you complicate the matter further, and unless there was something completely obvious as to why the decision changed, you will disrupt and confuse everyone around you.

Being decisive builds confidence amongst colleagues, subordinates, and bosses.

166

Hold On to Talent

The more turnover you have, the more expensive it is for you and the less competitive you will be. And that's just the beginning. The retention of talent and good employees is beyond the most important task you have. The attitude you have toward the issue of retention and the behavioral attitude you have toward your core talent will dictate the level of your success. Mismanage this part of your business or department, and watch your number go nowhere.

167

Think Before You Upgrade

Look at your P&L year-over-year. Guess what? The IT portion of your costs continues to rise. We all know how important technology is, but to what end? To what benefit? In other words, what is the reason and context for which you need it? There are so many questions you need to be asking with regard to technology, because it's expensive and it's supposed to be a time- and money-saver in the short and long term, allowing you to continually piggy-back off the technology and become more productive. Your questions must be detailed and your answers accurate. What is motivating you to upgrade or change your current technology? Where do you want it to take you? Know why you need it; otherwise, it's an expensive waste.

168

Challenge Yourself

It has to be one of the most difficult things to do. But if you don't challenge yourself, you will remain behind the pack—because others *are* doing it, and the further your peers get ahead, the greater the distance between you grows, the less competitive you become, and the less marketable you are. Challenging yourself gives you knowledge and experience. Without it, complacency is easy.

169

Sharpen Your Marketing

Marketing is a science, one of the most incredibly underestimated and undervalued in business. It goes to the core of our being, and when it's done in a sloppy or dull way, watch out—you're going nowhere fast. Your marketing skills (whether you are a marketer or not) need to be sharpened to the point of complete focus.

Let's take your business first. Send out a bunch of postcards hoping to get a callback, or run a television ad on whatever channel and wait by the phones, and you're not going to have much luck. Your research must be detailed and accurate as to whom you're targeting, otherwise you're wasting resources, including time and money. This sounds simple, right? Everyone should know this. But they don't. Even if they do, many market wrongly and lazily. If you sharpen your marketing efforts and continually focus and adjust, you will see the benefits.

On a personal level, you should be marketing yourself the same way as above. In everything you do, you are marketing yourself. Want to succeed? Sharpen the marketing of yourself.

170

Have a Purpose

It's a question that you should be asking yourself all of the time: "What is my purpose for doing this?" There has to be a reason. It's akin to cause and effect. If there is no particular purpose to doing something, then don't do it. There must be something on the other end; if not, an effort is suspicious and outright odd. Know what you are thinking. Ask the question.

171

Discipline Your Power

So much has been written about power. One of the most popular sayings is, "What does a man with power want? More power." It can be intoxicating. Power itself is not a bad thing, though. Of course it can be abused, and when that happens, others who are less powerful tend to suffer the most. However, disciplining your power or authority in a way that allows others to follow is very good. It's called leadership.

Discipline your power in a way that shows confidence, supports your staff, balances your disposition, allows you to be approachable, conveys authority without having to verbally correct, communicates direction accurately, and is strong when necessary and conciliatory when necessary. Discipline your power using some humility and balance, and your efforts and direction will be realized much more effectively and productively.

172

Find Trusted and Loyal Employees

Everyone has an agenda. So do you just hire people and hope for the best? Maybe not. There are three types of managers, and each has a specific approach.

1. *The one who doesn't say much:* This type of leader is usually more paranoid than others and can create distrust or insecurity among the staff, not allowing trust or loyalty to form.
2. *The one who talks too much:* This type of leader says too much to too many, not allowing anyone to quite trust him or her.
3. *The one who knows:* This type of leader understands when there is chemistry, talent, and ambition. He or she opens a relationship that is less dictatorial and more idea-driven. This is where you will find your trusted and loyal employees.

173

Things Change ... Be Ready

Are you comfortable? Everything stable and going your way? That's nice, but you had better get your résumé prepared. Things change, and when they do, it's usually not at the time you're expecting or in the way you would expect.

You need to be agile and prepared for abrupt changes in your career and life. Three of the most stressful changes in a person's life (outside the loss of a loved one) are:

1. A career or job change, whether voluntary or not
2. A physical move from one home to another home
3. A divorce or relationship abandonment

Be ready. If you are at least minimally aware that things change, you will be a little better prepared to handle things.

174

Engage in Creative Destruction

"Creative destruction" sounds contradictory, but it's not. The term describes an overreliance on creativity and unmanaged business sense. Believe me, creativity is good—if you have that, you are 80 percent there. However, not being able to channel and manage that creativity into something that brings in revenue will suck the life out of your financial resources and talent's morale. There's nothing like working hard on something and watching it go nowhere.

175

Don't Substitute Reliance for Knowledge

Reliance is okay in some circumstances, but it can be a crutch for a lack of knowledge or fear of making a decision. This goes to challenging yourself: don't allow yourself to be reliant on something just because it's the easiest thing to do at the moment. Not having the knowledge usually means you lack the experience.

Deferring knowledge to someone else is not good. Be careful of your reliance on others' decisions or the status quo that's always worked, alleviating you of having to gain the knowledge for yourself.

176

Understand that Your Experience Is Perishable

I will share two quick experiences of mine, and I'll bet that you will relate.

I can remember sitting in my marketing class at NYU as the professor began to compliment a student project. He was describing my project, although he did not have the project in his hand at the moment; he was describing it from memory. It was very flattering to me ... until he said, "I believe it was Roger's paper—nice job." All I remember thinking was, "What the hell?" (I never raised my hand to correct the professor—and neither did Roger, for that matter.)

More recently, I was in a meeting involving a large project when one of the people in the meeting said, "It was my idea to do this ..." Now, it was not this person's idea. I was the one who made the decision and implemented the change, whatever it was. Did I correct this person? No, why should or would I?

Again, the cemeteries are filled with indispensable people. Do not think for a moment that there is something that you are doing that no one else can do, or that the sun won't come up tomorrow because your experience is so great. Wrong. Life moves on, things move forward. What you say and do today is forgotten tomorrow. You must be aware that there is a continuum, and that your momentum cannot stop. Your experience is a perishable item. Continually look forward and renew.

177

Have a Reason for What You Are Doing

The best way to sap not only your morale but the morale of everyone around you is to show up with the same attitude and mundane approach to things. Why are you here today? What's the purpose of you showing up, and what are you looking to get out of this? What's the end result? Sapping morale is contagious, especially when you're in charge. That's not leading. There must be a reason you are doing something. Again, this goes to purpose—to challenging yourself, challenging the status quo. Do you want to increase morale? Show a direction, a benchmark, a goal, an objective. Low morale translates into one thing: low productivity.

178

Do What You Know

Okay, so you've heard that motivational thing, that you can accomplish anything you set your mind to. You can be anything you want. Now, you know that's not true. Honestly, who would believe that?

What do you know how to do? Again, we all have our equilibrium—what balances us, a talent, an attribute, whatever they may be. You probably have a good idea what you are good at. And that's the ticket. Do what you know how to do, and you will be happy. Happy means success. Not the success you read about in magazines, but real success, real happiness. When you are doing what you know, your confidence increases the productivity of your efforts. There's a deliberate but natural momentum.

179

Manage, Don't Maintain

This concept is very simple and will not take many words to describe. If you are not managing, you are maintaining. Maintaining is brainless. Managing takes thinking. Think about it this way… when you are mindlessly surfing the web or changing television channels without any plan or strategy you are simply maintaining a behavior that's getting the minimum done/accomplished. When you know what you are searching for, you' are going directly to it… or at least working your way to it, hence managing. So, the point is to manage issues with that intent, not to be satisfied with the status-quo and/or dealing with issues as they come up – that's not managing, that's maintaining.

180

Use Efficient Managing Strategies

When you have strategies, efficient managing comes naturally. Strategies are maps with a direction from point A to point B, and good ones will leave room for adjustments if necessary … and it will probably be necessary. The best battle plans go astray, and when management is efficient—meaning focused, intuitive, alert, having forethought, experienced, and knowledgeable—overall the objective or goal will be obtained in a much smoother way than if you're managing by the seat of your pants. Clear communication is key.

181

Organize Your Intentions

You must have intentions. You intend to reach that goal or intend to get that policy through. But how? Organizing your intentions means having a strategy to manage them. You can intend to do something, but if it's not thought through and contemplated, there's a good chance what you intend won't come out the way you intended. Remember that the worst ideas can be based on the best of intentions.

182

Be Prepared for the Aging Workforce

I'm sure you have heard much about the aging workforce. How does this affect your organization or the running of your department? First things first: it isn't necessarily a bad thing. With age comes experience and wisdom. The area of concern has more to do with change. Upgrades in technology or procedural changes may make an aging workforce timid or uncomfortable. Not many embrace change, especially when they've been doing something a certain way for a few decades.

An organization must be prepared for this by grasping the context internally. Additional training or coaching may be necessary. What happens often, unintentionally, is that blocking or sabotage will take place—only because there's insecurity, resistance, and fear of change. Things do not get done, questions are posed, and defensive behavior sets in. Again, it's not intentional. It's psychological.

I do concede that blocking and sabotage can be done by anyone, any age group … but I'm referring more to the impact that technology and procedural changes have. Honestly, have you ever watched a thirteen-year-old on a computer or an iPhone? There needs to be sensitivity to the issue and consideration with internal policies.

183

Avoid Lazy Thinking

Whatever you're working on, just get it done. It doesn't matter how. Well, that's not really true, or good for that matter. Lazy thinking means others are coming up with the ideas, not you. Your mind needs to keep moving forward; alternatively, it is just rethinking the same thoughts over and over. It does nothing for you. Lazy thinking is the mundane, everyday routine that keeps you in place and generates zero morale for yourself and others around you, including your boss, team, and colleagues. Lazy thinking is simply non-ideas, no creativity in your thought process, and a boring meltdown of your brain. Put a spark in your mind—ask lots of questions, work through the issues, know what you are thinking. Think! That's what your mind is for.

184

Build Your Ideas on Organized Thoughts

This is an efficiency tool. If you don't have your thoughts organized, everything after that won't be organized. So organize your thoughts and then begin building your ideas around those organized thoughts. In other words, you're bridging all the time. For example, you see something in the street, it gives you an idea of something else, and so on. I know it's a pain in the neck to do, but document the idea, because if you don't, you'll forget it for sure. Once you've gone through this process, begin implementation. You will find it much easier to implement when things are organized and strategized beforehand.

185

Understand Contentious Managers

You either have to work with contentious managers or work without them. Remember, you always have a choice. Let's start with working with them. If they are contentious, it could be for any number of reasons, most of which you may not care about. What you should do, with respect to yourself and within the context of your responsibilities, is find out exactly what's causing the contention when it comes to you. This is not so easy and may take time.

Having a contentious manager is bad for morale and creates tension where none is needed. It simply makes your job harder. Nevertheless, it's your responsibility to try to fix it or work with it in a productive way. It will be difficult if not impossible to have the contentious manager conform to you and everyone else. The only way to "fix" a contentious manager is to know and understand what he or she wants and how to adjust your habits or routines so that they are more in sync.

Making this work is your responsibility. However, this does not alleviate the manager's responsibility to be more approachable. The contentious behavior is to the manager's detriment and the detriment of the organization, as the performance of others will suffer. No one is going to want to bring in an idea or do something creative or risky only to be confronted in a contentious way.

Now, let me mention something about working without these troublesome managers. There's only one way to do it: leave your job. There's nothing else you can do. Your job does not owe you anything. Never think that it does. If you don't like the way things are—in this case, a contentious manager you have a hard time dealing with—then *you* leave. Easier said than done, I know, but that's also why you should always be prepared for change.

186

Remain Aloof to Some Issues

Not everything you do in your position is important. I'll take that even further: not everyone who has something to say to you is important either. You need to be able to disseminate what is important to you and what is not. Your aloofness to issues that are not going to advance your career or current project should be tolerated. You can put some interest or attention to it so you're not coming across as rude, but that's it. Go forward without giving it another thought.

Gossip, rumors, chit-chat, off-the-cuff comments … all can all be useful, but only if they don't waste your time. You need to be aloof to some of these issues to move forward.

187

Coordinate with Other Managers

Management cohesion must be in lockstep, to the point that, if one manager is asked a question, another manager will answer in the same way. I'm not talking about robotic and homogenized responses—I'm talking about no dissension or questioning of another to a line employee or outside contractor. Nothing poisons a strategy or an organization's culture more than dissension and fractured management. It is the opposite of efficiency, productivity, and a creative culture.

188

Beware Anxiety Paralysis

You've seen the image of a deer stuck in the headlights. It sees the light, it becomes mesmerized because it has no clue what's coming, and it freezes. Humans are the same. It happened to me once in the NYC subway system. I won't give you the details, but I experienced anxiety paralysis. I froze—and believe me, my friends were not happy.

This happens in a more subtle way in the workplace—and if it happens to you while you're working, you'd better exit to the restroom or something. I'm exaggerating ... but not completely. Anxiety paralysis happens when you're feeling insecure about a situation, or you're confused, or you simple freeze up (even if you know what to do), and the result is that you do nothing. By failing to engage or make a decision, you become stuck in the same place. Believe me, others notice. It's a sure way to be stepped over.

189

Tolerate Just Enough

We are all tolerant in one way or another. Dad will tolerate a messy room, Mom won't. Leaders need to be a little more discriminating as to what they will or won't tolerate. One thing is for sure: tolerating whatever just to keep the peace or because you're afraid of confrontation is not possible. Tolerance, or lack thereof, allows for guidelines. If anything is tolerated, risks become chaotic gambles, behavior becomes undisciplined, and the result is bad decisions. Tolerate just enough to allow your team or employees to grow, take chances, make some mistakes, and take risks.

190

Be Able to Explain Your Purchases

Purchasing is a key component in cost containment. The thing about numbers is that they add up very quickly—in either direction. So purchasing always needs to be watched with an eye on return and necessity. (You know how it is in negotiations—if you hear your opponents say that they "want" it, it's a lot different from saying they "need" it.) When purchasing, ask the question, "What's the return on this?" It does not always have to be monetary, and the return does not always have to be immediate, but there should be something that you can use to explain why you purchased it. The term *return on investment* (ROI) is a big one. It's what everyone in business is looking for. If it's not tangible enough for you to explain the purchase easily, then you probably shouldn't buy it. Buying just to buy puts money in others' pockets, not yours or your company's.

191

Weed Out Bad Employees Quickly

Regardless of the policies you have in place, HR's vetting, and stringent criteria to hire the right people, a dud can always slips through. The contagion this causes goes beyond any tangible monetary value lost or wasted on bad behavior. The behavior infects your bottom line and the customer's interactions with your company. There are many ways this can be handled. The worst way is an over-tolerance of the behavior, letting the individual do whatever in the belief that he or she will end up isolated. You hope. What's happening, in fact, is that your over-tolerance of the behavior is enabling that individual in a way that will only get worse and become more detrimental to your organization or team. The solution? Cut your losses and cut the employee loose, the sooner the better. Obviously, this is much more difficult in a protected union environment, but you need to start someplace with documentation so that when the union, EEOC, or Mr. Attorney comes asking questions, you have the answers.

There are all kinds of books, articles, and examples of workplace behavior and how to understand and deal with it. But why do you need to understand? What does it have to do with your business, and why should you care? Just make sure that your organization is organized to the point of being able to weed bad employees out quickly, legally, and permanently. An over-tolerance and attempt to "understand" will only delay the process, to your organization's detriment. It's not worth the energy.

192

Avoid Linear Thinking

Linear thinking basically means one-dimensional thinking. In other words, easy thoughts that don't change much from minute to minute or day to day. It's like the mindless process of surfing the Web or flicking through channels on the TV with no apparent goal. It just doesn't involve any exercise for the brain. You and your staff need to be inspired and motivated in thinking more two- or three-dimensionally. Take risks, discuss options, change a product, develop a creative department, get rid of nonperformers. Linear thinking will get you nowhere. It's lazy thinking.

193

Use New Hires to Change the Culture

I've mentioned culture a number of times in this book, and I cannot stress the importance of it and the positive or negative impact it can have on your organization or department.

Changing an organization's culture is extremely difficult. If your current culture is not productive to your organization, you need to change it from the top down and bottom up. This either demands inflating the payroll or letting people go, which can be a demoralizer and therefore counterproductive.

In any event, the strategy is to change the internal culture with a clear strategy for new hires. The assimilation process needs to work from the new to old, not the other way around; otherwise, your efforts are meaningless. It all comes down to your ideas on how it should be—your thoughts, contemplation, clear strategy, implementation, and maintenance. The battle will then be afoot like a tug of war. Your culture is vital to your success.

194

Pay Attention to Operations

In every organization, you have the operations arm. It's like the fluid that keeps all the moving parts working smoothly. Pay attention to operations and watch everything else run smoothly. Don't pay attention, don't invest in it, and watch the organization stutter and stumble. This has to do with everything from communications to logistics to the right software to the walking distance between key departments. When production and operations move right, everything moves right. Figure it out.

195

Support Key Managers

One of the basic responsibilities of a leader is to support key managers. It's a very big mistake, therefore, to undermine your managers' efforts. It's key that other staff members within the organization see this. Otherwise, dissension forms, and it's akin to trying to dig out of a deep hole after that.

The responsibility of the leader is to convey the direction or mission in a clear and concise way so there is no misunderstanding, and to have a clear understanding and confidence in their managers' ability, personality, efforts, and ambitions to follow through and manage in the context of the mission set forth. Again, that is the leader's responsibility. Failing at this will create dissension and mismanagement, and worse.

The responsibility of the manager is to understand all of the above. If a manager is a rebel, has a childish personality, is unable to follow direction or strategy, has grown stale or bored in the position, is not a team player, and thinks he or she is the smartest in the room ... in other words, if these individuals bring on the lack of or an undermining of support upon themselves, then they need to be pushed out.

Everyone wants to be in charge. Power can be intoxicating. But when a clear understanding of direction is not evident or not existing between a leader and his or her managers, things go wrong. Undermining support becomes a form of tension.

196

Anticipate Change ... and Resistance

Predictability and an anticipated result are probably two of the most comforting feelings you can have in business. But they really don't exist. The definition of managing is to set policies and procedures that are predictable. In other words, you do what you can so everyone knows what to do. The problem is that the best strategies or battle plans will go astray. Change is inevitable.

Change is going to bring resistance no matter how you describe it, prepare for it, or anticipate it. Therefore, whatever your changes are, whether anticipated or not, you must make adjustments in preparation for them. Resistance is absolutely normal and is literally part of the change itself.

The thing you need to figure out is how to make changes while minimizing the impact of resistance. One of those ways is to change the environment that resistant employees work within. In other words, instead of trying to change people, change the environment in which they work, allowing them to conform to the new environment more naturally.

197

Be Prepared to Be Devalued

You need to look at yourself closely all of the time. You are competing with others all of the time. Time does not stop, and you are either using the time to create value for yourself or time is using you. When it's the latter, all you end up with is wrinkled skin and regrets over what you would've, should've, could've. Yikes!

The skills that you learned in that expensive school may be a devalued five or ten years from now. The position you have grown into through your hard work and devotion may not be necessary with restructuring or technology. Your accomplishments can be put on your résumé, but your current position has used those accomplishments and continues to move forward … maybe needing you, maybe not.

Never put yourself in a position where you feel valued to the point of job security or "founder" security, for that matter. Your skills, position, and accomplishments are gone tomorrow. No one will care. Life moves at such a speed that there are a million more people coming right behind you. You must hold yourself in value only to the point of being prepared for that value to be gone. What will you do next? Are you prepared to be devalued?

198

Challenge Your Achievements and Goals

There's nothing like putting yourself into perspective. Have you ever challenged your achievements? Thought about how those achievements have brought you to where you are today? Are you able to stand on those achievements and continue to build?

How about your existing goals? Do you have any? If not, why not? Maybe you are just one of those people who is la-de-da-ing through life and hoping for the lottery to hit, without even playing it. Or maybe you do have goals? What's your strategy for reaching that goal, whatever it may be?

You need to challenge your accomplishments, your self, and your goals to determine whether you're fulfilled and happy with the way things are going. Life can be tough when it's not thought through and engaged. We all know it's a mistake to believe that everything is going to go the way you want it to, but it's also a mistake not to accept the challenge and try to get your way.

199

Know Where You Are

Just as you should know what you are thinking all of the time, you also should know where you are all of the time. This doesn't mean, "I'm on the corner of Main and Fourth Street." It means, where you are in the context of your position? How did you get there? Are you happy there? That self-awareness and understanding will help you beyond what you can imagine, because it will always force you to question yourself. And once you're questioning yourself, your mind begins to create options.

You know how important landmarks are. You need to have these landmarks in mind during your professional life. *This looks familiar, I've been here before, and what do I do now?* If you're aware of yourself, you know where you are in your professional life, and it is much easier to plan and strategize going forward. The opportunities only come when you are aware of them.

200

Drop Your Psychological Weight

Have you ever gotten that feeling when something is stuck in your head and you just can't free yourself of it? It's distracting; it fogs your thoughts and even freezes you in some cases. This is psychological weight, and in its worse form it can make you ineffective and unproductive. This weight can come from anything from problems at home to a bad run-in with the boss. Carrying it around will only exacerbate the situation, forcing you to malfunction. The neurons in your brain have no clue what to do, so what they do is focus on the problem, exaggerating your fears and interfering with your judgment. The solution? Well, we are all different ... that breath of fresh air or walk around the block may work for Joe, but it may not work for you.

This is when your mind really needs to be disciplined, and the issue creating the psychological weight must be managed in its proper context. Easier said than done, absolutely, but you need to find the formula that works for you and practice it. The alternative is that you'll go into a down mode, when you need to stay at your peak all of the time.

201

Figure Your Formula

You may have a formula without even realizing it. The very successful have figured out their formula and stick with it. There are things that you are doing wrong, and chances are you probably haven't figured out what's wrong with that formula either. This all comes down to being aware of yourself and the decisions you are making and what effect they are having. There must be an element of self-control.

In any event, ultimately, you need to figure out what is working for you and what is not.

202

Work on "the Vision Thing"

Vision is elusive to some. Your vision many times is imagined in your head, and it's not always easy to describe what your vision is. That said, the vision is the core, inspiration, and motivator that make things happen. It's the larger picture that needs to be broken down into its parts to make it happen.

Your vision of where you want to be tomorrow, five years from now, and beyond needs a focused strategy that is implemented day in and day out by you. Whether it's a personal vision or a business one, "the vision thing" is what you see and need to have. Breaking it down into pieces takes work and managing.

203

Think Things Through

Thinking is something we take for granted, because that's what we do naturally all the time. Issues, challenges, and problems come up constantly, and just thinking about them many times is not enough. Thinking through things to their end allows for a more predictable outcome. You have to contemplate, so all the variables become clear. This doesn't mean the outcome will always be to your satisfaction, but at a minimum, you've thought it through and anticipated all the possibilities.

204

Avoid Exaggerated Effort

Have you ever heard of the Law of Least Effort? It has to do with applying yourself just enough so things will come to you naturally. I'm not sure if that actuality works, but certainly exaggerating your efforts to the point of spinning your wheels or working harder than you should be applies here. Working exaggerated hours to look like you're working hard, or getting things done in a hurry for the sake of impressing your boss, is not the best strategy. Your efforts should move in a natural, concentrated, and deliberate way—smartly.

205

Define Your Course

Thorough definition of a policy, a vision, a strategy, or an understanding will allow you to decipher the intricacies of the direction. Organizing yourself and having a clear, anticipated result comes from the definition you give to the matter. How you define the above to yourself is how you perceive its result. Details matter to the point of success or failure. To not have your course defined is akin to relying on the ocean tides to land you at a certain parallel. Good luck with that strategy. Placing your attention on where you want to end up gives you a pretty good chance of getting there. Defining your course, anticipating challenges along the way, but maintaining your attention gives you an advantage over the many that simply allow the tides to take them.

206

Engage Yourself

It doesn't matter what the situation, challenge, problem, or issue is, if you're not engaged, then you're not engaged. If you don't discipline yourself, someone else will. When you don't engage yourself, your influence ceases to exist.

Engage yourself in what matters to you, in what will impact you. Growing leadership demands it.

207

Don't Confuse Learning with Experience

Just because you've learned something does not mean you have experience. You can learn anything, but the only way to gain actual knowledge is through experience. I understand that this sounds simple, however, how many résumés do you look at in which what is described as experience was actually learned from schooling? That's theoretical experience, if you can even call it that. No, experience is a physical, continued action in which variables become anticipated and expected. Learning is simply a base understanding of the concept. It gives you no experience whatsoever.

In this context, if you are hiring or promoting someone who has learned the new position through watching or from a degree, you had better be prepared to incubate the individual until he or she has gained the experience. If that individual believes, without humility, that learning is a qualification for the position, it will invite not only errors in judgment but also dissension among colleagues—especially the ones who *do* have experience. It's bad for morale.

208

Put Yourself in Gear

Where are you today? Where were you five years ago? Where will you be five years from now? You must measure yourself and determine whether you are stuck. If you find that you are bored, if you feel as though work has become a chore, if you're not learning anything new, if you continue with the same mundane pattern of drudgery day after day, then you are stuck.

At this point you need to engage yourself, put yourself in gear, and figure out something. There is nothing worse than watching a human being who is unhappy trying to make a living. When your mind begins to think of possibilities, opportunities flow. Also, your attitude will determine how others perceive you for those opportunities. Remember, we are social beings. We need each other. Are you stuck?

209

Stay Competitive

You've heard the expression that change is the only constant. It's true, and just as people are born every day, others are graduating college every year, and others are building their experience by working early in life. All of them continue to come through the ranks, changing the status quo, generating new ideas and new businesses. The influence you once had is shrinking all of the time. It's not a good or bad thing, it's just a thing that you should be aware of and attempt to manage.

How do you manage something like that? By being aware of your surroundings—including the people around you, technology changes, market changes, management changes, and board changes. This doesn't mean that you become Mr. or Mrs. Paranoia, but accepting that changes do take place and trying to stay ahead of the game by keeping yourself competitive is a good idea.

210

Work Your Way Up the Corporate Ladder, Not Down

Here's something you should look out for, even if you're being stepped over for promotion. One sure way to know that you're going the wrong way on the ladder of success is if newly created management positions are leaving you out. The more layers between you and your organizational head is an indication that you're working your way down the corporate latter, not up.

211

Don't Be Held Back

The relationship between you and your boss is important. I think that goes without saying. The truth is that if your relationship is not good with your boss for whatever reason, he or she can hold you back. Your boss needs to know that you are interested in moving up, that you want more responsibility.

We all have our need for security, so putting up with the lack of growth and the compensation rewards that come with it sometimes seems to be a default strategy. In other words, *I'll just deal with being held back for now and see what happens.* Is this a mistake? That's a question only you can answer, because you are the closest to yourself and understand your needs and wants better than anyone. However, not taking risks and allowing yourself to be held back by someone else is hard to explain to yourself later. Sometimes the grass *is* greener on the other side.

212

Measure What You Have, Where You Are, Where You Are Going

You have to be able to measure what you have, where you are, and where you are going. The truth of the matter is that you may be on the right track. Making a move out of dissatisfaction, impatience, or the thought that you're overqualified in your current position is just disruptive.

Measure yourself—and I mean *everything*, from your title to your fulfillment to your happiness to your struggle with bills to the kind of car you drive to your relationships both in and out of work. After doing that, ask yourself if you are in a good place. Once you've done that, do you know where you're going, or are you winging it?

The point here is to know where you are. Measure your situation before you make any moves. Sometimes the grass *isn't* greener on the other side.

213

Measure Your Productivity by What Makes You Happy

Time is beyond precious, and it's incredible how much time we waste on the mundane things—stupidity, gossip, mindless TV shows, lazy thinking, pointless actions. I could fill this whole book with examples. But, all in all, these things are just part of living, aren't they?

When I was a child, I couldn't wait until tomorrow. As an adult, I wish time would move more slowly. But that's not the answer, is it? It's what we do with our time and the productive manner in which we manage it that's important.

Your productivity is only measured by what makes you happy. That's the bottom line. Whether it's spending time with the kids, going to the bar with friends, working on Sundays, watching TV for downtime, taking a drive, riding your mountain bike, swimming ... you get the point. But even after all of that, there must be something you are adding in a productive way. Otherwise, time is wasted, and that's not good for you—career-wise or otherwise.

214

Understand Yourself and Your Intentions Toward Others

I've mentioned this before: we are social beings. This is why you look at others as you walk down the street, while you are on the subway or bus; it's why we have relationships. Regardless of the advances in technology, people will always be at the core. Facebook is a perfect example of technology based on social needs. Understanding your relationships, how you are intertwined with others, and how others perceive you will dictate how far you go. The intentions you have are more obvious to others than you may know, and the rapport you have with others is a determining factor of trust.

The way you perceive yourself is the way others will perceive you. Your actions are determined by who is around you. In other words, you act a certain way in front of different people based on your surroundings. Therefore, it is important that you know who you are and how you relate, and then translate that for others to understand your intentions, building trust and forming a rapport with individuals based on your mutual interests.

A lot of this sounds philosophical, and perhaps it is; however, in business and as a leader, it is critical to understand and practice your position among others. Accept this premise, or your boss and colleagues will not understand you. If you're not moving forward, you're not moving.

215

Pay Attention to the Big Things

If you're concentrating on small things, getting caught up in the day-to-day drudging maintenance of your work and ignoring the larger picture, then why would you expect anything greater from your current position? Certainly there are things that you must do on a day-to-day basis, but allowing them to absorb your working day will ensure that you stay at that level. Ignore the big things going on around you at your own peril; it will shut you down and force you to stay concentrated on the small things. Open yourself up, gain an interest in the bigger picture, and you'll start to see other possibilities and opportunities.

216

Always Be Looking for New Things

The best way to stagnate in an organization is to allow distractions to overtake you. Becoming obsessed with petty or manageable issues will slow any momentum.

In your organization or team, when a petty distraction creeps in, squash it as quickly as possible. Hoping that it will go away is not good enough. These things have a way of creating rumors that can either be demoralizing (again, slowing progress) or linger to the point of distracting good people from a more important objective. When the issue is more pressing, someone within the organization or your team should be assigned to deal with it so the rest of the team can continue forward without interruption.

An organization must always be looking for ways to move forward, new opportunities to help it compete, new ways to approach and handle customers, new processes for increased productivity. If distractions are allowed to persist or ferment, this slows and saps the organization's talent of its morale, creating a stagnant culture. Try competing with that.

217

Reject Petty Conditioning

In every organization, there is a culture. When people are in an organization for too long, they tend to become conditioned in a way that is not helpful to the organization. For example, "This is the way it's always been done," or "Bob has never been good at what he does here," or "Don't worry about that work." Petty conditioning is something that less-productive employees engage in to justify their low productivity and disinterest in their job or the organization as a whole.

You should know what to listen to and accept as useful to yourself and move on. The best strategy is to understand that it's simply petty, and any energy you put toward it will only trap you. Without realizing it, after a while you'll become a victim of petty conditioning, which doesn't help you to advance in the least.

218

Navigating Your Personal Growth

Your professional growth is what fulfills you. Your personality, your performance, your education, your character, your body language... it all plays a role, and then some.

The key is how you manage yourself within the context of your goals and objectives, and many times this is ignored in the place of, just trying to get by. That may be okay if that is what you want, but not if you are trying to grow professionally in an ever increasing competitive economy. Your niche to be good at something (not everything) is critical. Your approach and effort, and most importantly your ability to navigate yourself through the many obstacles (as listed in this book) is of paramount necessity. That corny phrase about your life being a journey is true for your professional growth. You are in phases, and if you allow your growth (or journey) to be dictated by others, then it will be.

About the Author

John Canavan was born, raised, and educated in New York City. He is an avid student of business philosophy and strategic planning. He currently works in the hospitality/ tourism trade, has owned and operated businesses in the United States and abroad, and has consulted for small businesses through FocuStrategy, concentrating on strategic planning and turnaround.

Mr. Canavan is the father of two children, a son and a daughter. He lives in Manhattan and leaves the island rarely.